A Report on the

Colllege Board Colloquium on

College Affordability
and Enrollment
Challenges

A Report on the

College Board Colloquium on
College Affordability
and Enrollment
Challenges

College Entrance Examination Board
New York, 1998

Founded in 1900, the College Board is a not-for-profit educational association that supports academic preparation and transition to higher education for students around the world through the ongoing collaboration of its member schools, colleges, universities, educational systems and organizations.

In all of its activities, the Board promotes equity through universal access to high standards of teaching and learning and sufficient financial resources so that every student has the opportunity to succeed in college and work.

The College Board champions—by means of superior research: curricular development; assessment; guidance, placement, and admission information; professional development; forums; policy analysis; and public outreach—educational excellence for all students.

Contents

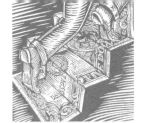

Introduction

The past several months have seen great media and government attention directed toward college costs. As more and more colleges have turned away from a standard need analysis and aid award philosophy, families and lawmakers have become concerned about the affordability of a college education. What drives college costs? How will the Taxpayer Relief Act of 1997 and other programs impact families and colleges? What is happening to the idea of access and opportunity for all? How can colleges cope with — or even overcome — enrollment challenges related to college costs? How can we as financial aid, admission, and counseling professionals help families prepare to pay for college?

To address college affordability and related issues — and to begin to work toward a consensus on addressing the needs of families and institutions in today's competitive climate — the College Scholarship Service Council (CSSC) and its Financial Aid Standards and Services Advisory Committee (FASSAC) sponsored the College Board Colloquium on College Affordability and Enrollment Challenges, January 11 and 12, 1998, in Chandler, Arizona.

The colloquium gave College Scholarship Service Assembly members — financial aid administrators and high school counselors, as well as admission and enrollment officers, an opportunity to examine together the complex issues surrounding college affordability, and how these issues are played out in the challenge of enrolling students. The 160 professionals who attended had the opportunity to engage in lively discussion about the challenges they face in relation to college costs. Experts in the economics of higher education, effective higher education management, government relations, and other areas helped provide a context for discussion.

We at the College Board hope that the colloquium and the following proceedings will encourage continued dialogue about

college affordability. This third annual financial aid colloquium reflects the Board's commitment to providing a forum for the discussion of complex issues; we stand ready to help members implement consensus-based positions as they develop.

We would also like to acknowledge and thank the following people whose gifts of time, talent, and enthusiastic support ensured the colloquium's success:

Joseph Allen, *vice provost for Enrollment and dean of Admission and Financial Aid, University of Southern California*

Stephanie Balmer, *director of Admission, Agnes Scott College*

Sandy Baum, *professor of Economics, Skidmore College*

Nancy Beane, *college counselor, The Westminster Schools, Atlanta*

Edwin Below, *director of Financial Aid, Wesleyan University, and chair, Financial Aid Standards and Services Advisory Committee*

Steven E. Brooks, *executive director, North Carolina State Education Assistance Authority, and College Board Trustee*

Frank Campanella, *executive vice president, Boston College*

John Curtice, *assistant vice chancellor for Student Affairs and Financial Aid Services, State University of New York*

Rebecca Dixon, *associate provost of University Enrollment, Northwestern University*

Mary Garren, *associate director, Scholarships and Student Aid, University of North Carolina, Chapel Hill*

Katharine Hanson, *president, COFHE*

Natala Hart, *director of Financial Aid, The Ohio State University*

Scott Healy, *director of Admissions, The Ohio State University*

Mark Lindenmeyer, *director of Financial Aid, Loyola College*

Lois Mazzuca, *college coordinator, Glenbrook North High School, Illinois*

Joseph Merante, *associate vice president for Academic Affairs, Loyola Marymount University*

James Miller, *director of Financial Aid, Harvard and Radcliffe Colleges*

Nancy Monnich, *director of Admissions and coordinator of Financial Aid, Bryn Mawr College*

James Morley, *president, NACUBO*

Walter Moulton, *director of Student Aid, Bowdoin College*

Mary Nucciarone, *director of Financial Aid, Saint Mary's College*

Shirley Ort, *associate vice chancellor and director of Scholarships, University of North Carolina, Chapel Hill*

Bernard Pekala, *director of Financial Aid, Boston College*

Thomas Rajala, *director of Admission, Boston University*

Donald A. Saleh, *dean of Admissions and Financial Aid, Cornell University, and chair, College Scholarship Service Assembly, and College Board Trustee*

Joellen Silberman, *dean of Enrollment, Kalamazoo College*

Myra B. Smith, *director of Financial Aid, Smith College*

Laurice "Penny" Sommers, *college counselor, John C. Fremont High School, Los Angeles, and College Board Trustee*

Diane Stemper, *director of Student Financial Aid, Miami University*

James M. Swanson, *director of Financial Aid, Colorado College*

Marcelle Tyburski, *director of Student Aid, Colgate University*

William Young, *director of Enrollment Management, Colorado School of Mines*

Last but not least, thanks are due to College Board staff members Kathleen Little, executive director of Financial Aid Services, and Clavel Camomot and Ron Barber, staff assistants, for their roles in the planning and implementation of the colloquium, and to Deb Thyng Schmidt, consultant to the College Scholarship Service, for her assistance in the preparation of this report.

Hal Higginbotham

Vice President
Student Assistance Services

Welcoming Comments

Donald A. Saleh, dean of Admissions and Financial Aid at Cornell University and chair of the CSS Assembly, opened the 1998 colloquium by expressing delight at seeing "so many people here who are willing to take the time from their busy schedules to share with each other their ideas and concerns on the issue of college affordability." Saleh indicated that he expected the weekend to be rewarding and productive, providing "a variety of perspectives to help us all work toward a better understanding of the impact of family perspectives about college affordability on colleges' enrollment efforts."

Saleh said that the higher education enrollment and financial aid arena has never been more complicated. In addition to the cost and competition factors with which institutions have been grappling for a number of years, there is the added twist of new tax legislation that will have an impact on how families approach paying for college. "As we move into this new playing field, it will be important to keep institutional and societal goals in mind, as well as the goals of students and families," he added. Saleh urged the colloquium to serve as a starting point for ongoing discussions — on the participants' campuses and in the associations — regarding college affordability. Saleh then introduced Donald Stewart, president of the College Board, thanking him and all those at the College Board and College Scholarship Service who helped put the colloquium together.

Donald Stewart welcomed all the participants on behalf of the College Board and its Trustees, and reiterated Saleh's thanks for the time the participants were taking to deal with "these issues without easy answers." Stewart indicated that the Board was proud to host the colloquium, because the Board sees its role "in facilitating discussions that can help develop solutions."

Stewart acknowledged the "rising level of expertise" that is being required of enrollment and financial aid professionals as they work to address the "complex and compelling" issues

1

related to affordability. As colleges are increasingly looking to families to cover higher costs, Stewart cautioned that we need to be aware that the aid to cover these costs has not similarly increased, and only the top income sector has seen real income growth. "In a competitive environment, where colleges are targeting their recruitment efforts to those who can pay, lower-income students may be the losers," he said.

Stewart suggested to the group that "first, we need to cope with the changing aid environment, and then decide how we will lead on the issue of need-based aid." He encouraged the group to "advance the cause of fair and equitable access, and to determine how to help those who will *not* benefit from the tax-law changes." In closing, Stewart assured the group that the College Board is involved in these issues as a "cooperative associational laboratory," and that the Board stands ready to help translate the needs and concerns addressed by the colloquium into workable solutions.

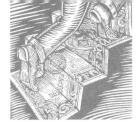

College Affordability and Enrollment Challenges

The keynote address for the colloquium was given by Dr. Michael McPherson, president of Macalester College, and Dr. Morton Schapiro, professor of Economics and dean of the College of Letters, Arts, and Sciences at the University of Southern California. Their remarks were based on their new book, *The Student Aid Game: Meeting Need and Rewarding Talent in American Higher Education.* Schapiro focused on changes in sources of revenue for higher education, and the impact of these changes on affordability and choice for students and families of different income groups. McPherson spoke about changes in financial aid policy at the institutional and governmental levels and the challenges related to a recommitment to need-based financial aid.

Schapiro began by giving "a long view of revenue sources for American higher education." He pointed out that the total bill for higher education in the United States is over $200 billion annually, or about 3 percent of the gross domestic product for the country. "We are an enormous industry."

In Table 1, *Shares of Higher Education Revenue,* Schapiro and McPherson have provided two basic categories of revenue sources for higher education — gross tuition revenue and nontuition revenue — and then shown more particularly where the money has come from for each category. Schapiro explained that the state and federal components on the tuition side include Pell Grants and other grants; federal revenues in the nontuition category are chiefly research monies paid to universities; and state and local grants are public institution appropriations. As Schapiro explained, "There have been some really amazing changes in revenue sources over a relatively short period of time. For example, who paid the lion's share of all the revenues to support higher education in 1979-80? State and local grants — primarily operating subsidies — while gross tuition accounted for only 26 percent of total revenue for higher education. Yet by

Table 1. Shares of Higher Education Revenue, by Source, Selected Academic Years, 1939-1993 (%)

| Academic Year | Gross Tuition | SOURCES OF GROSS TUITION REVENUE | | | | NONTUITION REVENUE | | |
		Families	Institutions	Federal Government	State Government	Federal Grants	State and Local Grants	Gifts and Endowment Earnings
1939-40	0.37	0.35	0.02	0.00	0.00	0.07	0.33	0.21
1949-50	0.40	0.37	0.03	0.00	0.00	0.12	0.32	0.12
1959-60	0.26	0.22	0.03	0.00	0.01	0.23	0.34	0.13
1965-66	0.26	0.21	0.04	0.00	0.01	0.26	0.33	0.09
1969-70	0.25	0.20	0.04	0.00	0.01	0.22	0.38	0.08
1975-76	0.26	0.16	0.04	0.04	0.02	0.20	0.43	0.08
1979-80	0.26	0.14	0.04	0.06	0.02	0.19	0.43	0.09
1985-86	0.29	0.17	0.05	0.05	0.02	0.16	0.41	0.10
1989-90	0.31	0.19	0.05	0.05	0.02	0.16	0.37	0.10
1991-92	0.34	0.22	0.05	0.05	0.02	0.16	0.35	0.10
1992-93	0.35	0.22	0.06	0.05	0.02	0.16	0.33	0.10

Notes: 1992-93 data are preliminary. Both veterans' educational benefits and social security benefits paid to qualified college students are excluded from federal tuition payments.

Sources: McPherson and Schapiro 1991b, p. 23; National Center for Education Statistics 1995a, tab. 318; College Board 1995, tab. 1.

McPherson, Michael, and Morton Schapiro; *The Student Aid Game: Meeting Need and Rewarding Talent in American Higher Education.* Copyright © 1998 by Princeton University Press. Reprinted by permission of Princeton University Press.

1992-93, the number-one source of higher-education revenue was gross tuition, at 35 percent; state and local grants had fallen amazingly quickly, from providing 43 percent to 33 percent of the total revenue."

Yet Schapiro indicated that if we take the long view, we see that this "is not a whole new world — it goes back to the old world." The current situation is not all that different from that of 1939-40, when the percentages of higher education revenue provided by state and local grants and tuition were almost identical to the percentages for those categories in 1993. Between 1939-40 and 1992-93, there was "a steady decline through 1980 in the overall share of tuition paid by families, the result of an increase in the enrollment share of public institutions, the growth of federal grants and contracts, and the rise in financial aid. The decline in the share of higher-education revenues provided by families came to an abrupt halt in the 1980s, with the family share increasing 8 percentage points in the 1980–93 period. Almost all this increase

in tuition revenue in the past fifteen years has been paid for by families; we do not find major increases in the percentage of gross tuition covered by the institutions themselves or by the government."

Next, referring to Table 2, *Financing of Undergraduate Tuitions,* Schapiro noted, "The natural question, when we look at families paying a much higher percentage of total revenues, is: Are we holding needy students harmless? Hopefully, it is the affluent students who can really afford it who are paying these increased costs." This table uses National Postsecondary Student Aid Surveys (NPSAS) data from 1986-87 and from 1992-93. The chart shows a $3,300 increase in gross tuition in adjusted dollars for low-income students at private institutions between 1987 and 1993. As it turns out, only about $1,000 of the gross tuition increase for low-income students was covered by sources other than the family (mainly, by the institutions themselves) because, for the low-income group, state grants went down, federal loans increased very little, and federal grants stayed approximately the same. Thus, the price (or net tuition) low-income students paid increased by $2,300 in real dollars over this relatively short period of time. While the net tuition price for more affluent groups went up even more, Schapiro pointed out that, given the sensitivity of the low-income group to even small price increases, "this is very worrisome."

What happened during this time at public institutions, where about 80 percent of all students go and the highest percentage of low-income students go? The sticker price (gross tuition) in percentage terms went up much more rapidly at public institutions, though the real dollar increase was only about one third of that at private institutions. The net tuition increase (after all types of aid were applied) at public institutions from 1986-87 to 1992-93 for low-income students in adjusted dollars was $800. "As recently as 1986-87, if we were to take the sticker price and

Table 2. Financing of Undergraduate Tuitions, 1986-87 and 1992-93 (in 1992-93 dollars)

Family Income Category		Net Tuition	Federal Grants	Federal Loan Subsidies	State Grants	Institutional Grants	Gross Tuition
PRIVATE NONPROFIT INSTITUTIONS							
LOW	1986-87	1,372	1,585	958	1,354	1,780	7,049
	1992-93	3,619	1,628	1,141	982	2,942	10,312
MIDDLE	1986-87	4,048	355	840	582	1,754	7,579
	1992-93	7,704	184	750	328	2,919	11,886
HIGH	1986-87	7,390	117	317	92	719	8,635
	1992-93	11,622	23	304	55	1,388	13,391
PUBLIC INSTITUTIONS							
LOW	1986-87	-439	980	370	355	168	1,434
	1992-93	360	1,051	489	352	267	2,520
MIDDLE	1986-87	1,030	97	278	102	154	1,661
	1992-93	2,113	84	220	85	263	2,765
HIGH	1986-87	1,721	37	73	18	83	1,932
	1992-93	3,112	11	84	38	193	3,437
PRIVATE FOR-PROFIT INSTITUTIONS (PROPRIETARY SCHOOLS)							
LOW	1986-87	1,124	1,546	1,233	266	70	4,238
	1992-93	4,155	1,254	1,102	122	69	6,702
MIDDLE	1986-87	3,281	180	1,245	207	105	5,018
	1992-93	5,842	94	784	69	110	6,898
HIGH	1986-87	4,630	33	349	27	62	5,102
	1992-93	6,852	7	188	0	25	7,071

Note: Numbers are averages across all full-time, dependent students attending a particular institutional type.
Source: Calculated from 1986-87 and 1992-93 NPSAS data bases.

INCOME GROUP	1986-87	1992-93
LOW	< $23,500	< $30,000
MIDDLE	$23,500 – $54,900	$30,000 – $70,000
HIGH	> $54,900	> $70,000

These income brackets are equivalent in 1992-93 dollars, reflecting the 27.6 percent increase in prices between the academic years being compared.

McPherson, Michael, and Morton Schapiro; *The Student Aid Game: Meeting Need and Rewarding Talent in American Higher Education.* Copyright © 1998 by Princeton University Press. Reprinted by permission of Princeton University Press.

discount it by institutional aid and various grants and subsidies, financial aid would have covered more than the cost of public institution tuition for low income students, and the excess would have been applied to the other costs of attendance, such as room

and board. By 1992-93, aid sources do not even cover tuition alone — a big change in a relatively short period of time," Schapiro said.

He added, "There is quite a large body of literature on the 'price elasticity of demand': how responsive consumers from different income brackets are to price changes in terms of their enrollment decisions. The data suggest that affluent and even middle-income students aren't very responsive to increases of the type that we have experienced so far. On the other hand, there is very strong data to suggest that for lower-income students, an increase of as little as $150 is significant: it will lead to about a 1.5 percent decline in enrollment rates. So when you look at these kinds of numbers, you have to be worried about the relationship between college costs and access and choice."

Schapiro explained that price is not the sole determinant of enrollment rates. Over this same period of time, the financial return to the student with a college degree has dramatically increased. Students who graduated from college in 1980 could expect to earn about 50 percent more over the course of their lifetimes than those who stopped with a high school degree. By 1998, a college graduate could expect to earn twice as much as a student with only a high school degree. This change in return can explain in part the increase in college enrollment in the face of rising net costs. Schapiro remarked, "This is the good news — but the bad news is that two thirds of this increase is due to the *decline* in what a person with a high school degree can earn rather than an *increase* in what a person with a college degree can earn."

Access to higher education is of even greater concern because noncollege graduates will lose out in the U.S. labor market. In referring to Table 3, *College Enrollment Rates of High School Graduates,* Schapiro pointed out that in 1980, there was indeed a gap between various groups going to college, but it was not a large gap: the gap between whites and African Americans was 5

Table 3. College Enrollment Rates of High School Graduates (%)

YEAR	WHITES	AFRICAN AMERICANS	THREE-YEAR AVERAGE	HISPANICS	THREE-YEAR AVERAGE
1960	45.8	—	—	—	—
1961	49.5	—	—	—	—
1962	50.6	—	—	—	—
1963	45.6	—	—	—	—
1964	49.2	—	—	—	—
1965	51.7	—	—	—	—
1966	51.7	—	—	—	—
1967	53.0	—	—	—	—
1968	56.6	—	—	—	—
1969	55.2	—	—	—	—
1970	52.0	—	—	—	—
1971	54.0	—	—	—	—
1972	49.4	—	—	—	—
1973	48.1	—	—	—	—
1974	47.1	—	—	—	—
1975	51.2	—	—	—	—
1976	48.9	41.9	—	52.6	—
1977	50.7	49.6	45.7	51.3	48.9
1978	50.1	45.7	46.9	42.9	46.3
1979	49.6	45.4	44.3	44.8	46.8
1980	49.9	41.8	43.4	52.7	49.9
1981	54.6	42.9	40.4	52.1	49.3
1982	52.0	36.5	39.3	43.1	49.8
1983	55.0	38.5	38.4	54.3	47.3
1984	57.9	40.2	40.3	44.3	49.9
1985	59.4	42.3	39.7	51.1	46.6
1986	56.0	36.5	43.6	44.4	43.0
1987	56.6	51.9	44.5	33.5	45.0
1988	60.7	45.0	49.9	57.0	48.6
1989	60.4	52.8	48.0	55.4	53.2
1990	61.5	46.3	48.2	47.3	53.3
1991	64.6	45.6	46.6	57.1	53.1
1992	63.4	47.9	49.7	54.8	58.1
1993	62.8	55.6	51.5	62.5	55.4
1994	63.6	50.9	—	48.9	—

Note: Enrollment rates reflect enrollment in college as of October of each year for individuals age 16 to 24 who graduated from high school (including GED recipients) during the preceding 12 months.

Source: Based on data in the *Digest of Education Statistics 1995*, National Center for Education Statistics 1995a, tab. 177.

percentage points, and between whites and Hispanics, about 3 percentage points. But by the mid-nineties, these gaps in enrollment had more than doubled.

Schapiro then told the group that, looking explicitly at income levels in 1980, 69 percent of students from families in the top income bracket went to college within twelve months of high school graduation (now it is 75 percent); 45 percent of students in the middle income group (25–75 income percentiles) went to college (now 50 percent), while enrollment from students in the lowest income group has remained steady at 26 percent. "This was a rather staggering difference in the college-going rate even in 1980, and now it is much worse." Schapiro noted that this gap is not surprising, given what was going on at the same time in terms of income: between 1980 and 1995, the average real income of the bottom 20 percent in the income distribution *decreased* by 9 percent, while the average real income for earners in the top 20 percent *increased* by an average of 2 percent per year. "The growing gap by race and income is indeed worrisome in terms of access," he said.

Another unsettling trend was discussed in reference to Table 4, *Freshman Enrollment, by Income Background, Across Institution Types.* Schapiro indicated that there is a very positive correlation between family income and attendance at a university: higher-income students are more likely to attend a public or private university than a college (one out of eight low-income students versus one out of two among the richest). "When you look at community colleges, you see exactly the opposite of the phenomenon you see for universities." The probability of attending a community college is strongly *negatively* associated with income. Almost half of the lower-income students (full-time, first-time students) enrolled in higher education in 1994 were enrolled in community colleges: one in two versus one in twelve of the highest income group. For all income groups except the

Table 4. Freshman Enrollment by Income Background Across Institutional Types (%)

INSTITUTION TYPE	INCOME BACKGROUND						
	LOWER	LOWER MIDDLE	MIDDLE	UPPER MIDDLE	UPPER	RICHEST	ALL GROUPS
1994							
PRIVATE UNIVERSITY	2.6	3.3	3.9	6.6	13.2	22.4	5.7
FOUR-YEAR COLLEGES	12.8	15.3	16.6	18.4	22.2	27.3	17.1
TWO-YEAR COLLEGES	3.1	2.9	2.5	2.2	2.8	3.8	2.7
ALL PRIVATE	18.5	21.5	23.0	27.2	38.2	53.5	25.5
PUBLIC UNIVERSITY	10.9	14.5	18.1	24.9	27.8	24.6	19.1
FOUR-YEAR COLLEGES	23.2	24.6	25.2	25.9	20.1	13.3	24.1
TWO-YEAR COLLEGES	47.3	39.4	33.7	22.1	13.9	8.6	31.3
ALL PUBLIC	81.4	78.5	77.0	72.9	61.8	46.5	74.5
TOTAL	100.0	100.0	100.0	100.0	100.0	100.0	100.0
1980							
PRIVATE UNIVERSITY	2.2	2.9	3.9	6.8	12.8	19.8	5.2
FOUR-YEAR COLLEGES	13.4	15.1	15.8	17.7	25.2	31.7	16.8
TWO-YEAR COLLEGES	5.6	5.1	3.7	3.3	2.6	2.5	4.0
ALL PRIVATE	21.2	23.1	23.4	27.8	40.6	54.0	26.0
PUBLIC UNIVERSITY	10.1	13.2	17.4	24.6	26.6	19.6	18.1
FOUR-YEAR COLLEGES	22.8	21.3	20.4	20.1	15.6	11.9	20.2
TWO-YEAR COLLEGES	45.9	42.4	38.9	27.6	17.3	14.5	35.8
ALL PUBLIC	78.8	76.9	76.7	72.3	59.5	46.0	74.1
TOTAL	100.0	100.0	100.0	100.0	100.0	100.0	100.0

INCOME GROUP	1980	1994
LOWER	<$10,000	<$20,000
LOWER MIDDLE	$10,000 – $15,000	$20,000 – $30,000
MIDDLE	$15,000 – $30,000	$30,000 – $60,000
UPPER MIDDLE	$30,000 – $50,000	$60,000 – $100,000
UPPER	$50,000 – $100,000	$100,000 – $200,000
RICHEST	>$100,000	>$200,000

Source: Calculated from results from the American Freshman Survey.

lowest income group, the probability of attending community college declined. "So, not only are low-income students adversely affected in terms of access, but their choices are

increasingly restricted. For many low-income students, the local community college is their only choice for beginning higher education, and that statement is truer now than it has been in the past. If you ask what percent of first-time, full-time students who begin higher education at a community college earn a baccalaureate degree, the answer is only 10 to 12 percent. That was true in 1980 and is true now." While this is not the mission of community colleges, it is still troubling that low-income students have been restricted in terms of choice.

Table 4 also provides information about what has been happening with middle-income families. The media have said for ten years that "middle-income students are bailing out of private colleges because they can't afford them: the colleges charge too much and the families are too rich for financial aid." Schapiro pointed out that there is absolutely no evidence to support this trend in the data. Private institutions have held their own with students from middle-income families; it is the *richest* families whose students are bailing out. All but the most elite private institutions are losing their full-paying students; the elite universities have maintained or even increased their share of the richest students.

In conclusion, Schapiro urged admission and financial aid officers "not to lose sight of the goals of need-based aid despite these pressures and the competition. As colleges and universities try to act more like businesses, we need never to lose the sense that we are different, that we are nonprofit, that we have certain responsibilities."

McPherson then addressed the group, reinforcing Schapiro's sense that the "trends as we see them are of concern. The forces that are hammering at higher education have been pretty severe in the past fifteen or twenty years." He added, "I do not think the idea that we are in a crisis, a critical turning point, is exaggerated." He indicated that competitive pressures that

Table 5. Admission Profile, Conjectural University

Combined SAT® Score	NO NEED			LOW NEED (Grant: 0-$5,000)			MEDIUM NEED (Grant: $5,000-$12,500)			HIGH NEED (Grant: $12,500-$25,000)			TOTAL		
	Apply	Accept	Enroll	Apply	Accept	Enroll	Apply	Accept	Enroll	Apply	Accept	Enroll	Apply	Accept	Enroll
1300+	75	75	20	75	75	25	75	75	30	60	60	30	285	285	105
1100-1300	125	110	40	125	110	45	125	110	50	125	110	60	500	440	195
900-1100	300	250	75	300	250	80	300	250	90	300	250	100	1200	1000	345
700-900	300	200	80	300	200	80	300	200	80	300	200	90	1200	800	330
Below 700	400	10	9	400	10	9	400	10	9	400	10	9	1600	40	36
TOTAL	1200	645	224	1200	645	239	1200	645	259	1185	630	289	4785	2565	1011
Average SAT Score	866	1018	988	866	1018	1003	866	1018	1015	858	1008	1013	864	1016	1011

McPherson, Michael, and Morton Schapiro; *The Student Aid Game: Meeting Need and Rewarding Talent in American Higher Education.* Copyright © 1998 by Princeton University Press. Reprinted by permission of Princeton University Press.

institutions are dealing with have led to the "erosion of commitment" to the standards of need analysis and need-based aid and toward new, complex strategies. This erosion is taking place at all levels: institutional, state, and federal.

McPherson referred the group to Table 5, which portrays an admission data analysis for an imagined university practicing need-blind admissions, with full-need funding of enrolled students and no merit aid. He explained that Conjectural University's data reflect a "plausible premise" for a university with this type of aid policy: that highly qualified students are more likely to be accepted and less likely to enroll, while higher-need students who are admitted are more likely to enroll. This type of table "allows you to crystallize the kind of trade-offs that are involved when you change admission and financial aid policies."

McPherson then led the group through an example based on the supposition that Conjectural University needs to save money in its aid operation, moving from a need-blind strategy to a need-aware one. McPherson explained that the scenario played out in Table 6 is "more dramatic than an institution would be likely to take": Conjectural University has decided to save aid dollars by

Table 6. Revised Admission Policy, Conjectural University

Combined SAT Score	NO NEED (Grant: 0-$5,000)			LOW NEED (Grant: $5,000-$12,500)			MEDIUM NEED (Grant: $5,000-$12,500)			HIGH NEED (Grant: $12,500-$25,000)			TOTAL		
	Apply	Accept	Enroll	Apply	Accept	Enroll	Apply	Accept	Enroll	Apply	Accept	Enroll	Apply	Accept	Enroll
1300+	75	75	20	75	75	25	75	75	30	60	60	30	285	285	105
1100-1300	125	125	45	125	110	45	125	110	50	125	110	60	500	455	200
900-1100	300	300	90	300	250	80	300	250	90	300	250	100	1200	1050	360
700-900	300	250	100	300	200	80	300	200	80	300	0	0	1200	650	260
Below 700	400	75	68	400	10	9	400	10	9	400	0	0	1600	95	86
TOTAL	1200	825	323	1200	645	239	1200	645	259	1185	420	190	4785	2535	1011
Average SAT Score	866	974	910	866	1018	1003	866	1018	1015	858	1117	1134	864	1020	1001

not admitting any of the highest-need, lowest-scoring (900 or below) applicants, which would cut enrollment by 99. Then, to maintain enrollment, they would admit (1) all no-need applicants with scores above 900 (2) 50 of the no-need applicants whose scores were between 700 and 900, and (3) as many no-need applicants with scores below 700 as needed to replace the remainder of the 99. This "aggressively need-aware" strategy would save $1.75 million the first year and $7 million a year once it was fully implemented. "But at what cost?" McPherson asked. In part, it would be in the academic quality of the class. By one measure, that doesn't seem to have had a large negative effect: the SAT average for the whole class would only go down five points, from 1006 to 1001. On the other hand, adding 50 students with scores below 700 may seem to have a very negative effect from the faculty's point of view.

McPherson said that a lot of colleges are debating the question, "Is this kind of change worth it?" Institutions are evaluating changes in strategy in terms of their educational goals and curricular goals, their ethical commitment (what are their responsibilities to high-need students who in other ways are more qualified than the students they would admit instead?) and to their strategic vision. "As these debates go on, it is clear that

more schools are opting in favor of policies like the need-aware admission policy I've described — though usually in more temperate and complicated forms. One consequence of that trend is that colleges choosing to remain need-blind and meet full need come under more pressure as a result of the changes other institutions make." As more schools become need-aware, the high-need students they turn away are more likely to enroll at colleges with need-blind policies, in turn making those policies more expensive and causing those institutions to look into need-aware policies as well. Schools are also looking at merit aid to increase their ability to enroll high-quality students, which puts pressure on colleges without merit aid since low-need, high-ability students are being enticed by other colleges. In addition to these trends, colleges are adopting increasingly aggressive differential packaging policies in the aid that is offered.

"It's very important not to be overly moralistic about these changes," McPherson stated, "because the plain fact is that circumstances alter cases. The difference is not the moral fiber of the leadership of institutions." Rather, it is that endowment levels and the family income of the typical applicant varies by institution. Colleges shouldn't be expected "to honor an abstract moral commitment at the expense of being able to fund the instructional program." At the same time, there is "a real issue about morality that comes into play: if you have a lot of resources, you should have a clear sense of the moral vision that allows you to justify merit aid or need-aware admission policies. And, as a moral bottom line, it is important to be honest about the policies you do have." There are policies that would be self-defeating if they were announced (for example, leveraging students who are most interested in a particular institution).

McPherson noted that the pressures colleges face are also being felt at the state and federal levels. At the state level, Georgia's

Hope Scholarships, for example, "are a very explicit attempt to walk away from helping students on the basis of need and target resources to middle-income students." McPherson believes the strong trend toward state prepaid tuition plans is "fed by an ill-conceived federal tax subsidy for such plans"; these plans move state dollars away from need-based aid. And at the federal level, the new tax-credit programs will become bigger in cost than federal Pell Grant or federal loan programs. The flap about whether to factor in the tax credit when doing need analysis exemplifies how college administrators are under tremendous pressure to ignore the tax credit when determining how much a family should pay and how to award their own aid resources. "To ignore the tax credit flies flatly in the face of the principles of need analysis," McPherson said.

He continued, "The very fact that people are so comfortable about pressing for this exception to standard need analysis underlines what bad shape need analysis is in as an evaluative basis for how we support the education of students." McPherson quoted Hegel, who, in writing about history, stated, "the owl of Minerva flies only at dusk" (i.e., wisdom and understanding of an era come only at the end of that era). "We are coming to understand need analysis and need-based aid only as they are ending," he said. These ideas were the organizing principles fifteen or twenty years ago: federal and state governments and institutions worked together to meet a commonly defined need. There was tension within this framework, but the framework focused energy and attention. "Now," McPherson conceded, "everyone is going after his own best interests, with federal and state governments looking to whom they can please politically and institutions looking at their own bottom lines."

McPherson wonders if this commitment to need-based aid can be recovered, or if we need to think of some new framework to impose discipline and common purpose. "I am really uncertain

about the answer to this question. If we do need a new framework, Morty [Schapiro] and I have had no success in imagining one that that would be as effective in managing limited resources as the need-based system is." McPherson concluded that the best hope would be the recommitment by the federal government to need-based aid, both through its own programs and through rewarding states and institutions that adhere to need-based aid practices.

The audience then had a chance to respond. Joe Russo, director of Financial Aid at the University of Notre Dame, asked, "Can we look for some good in the taxpayer relief legislation by trying to strengthen the best part, that more families can do a better job of planning for and saving for college?" He wondered if we could work together toward moving beyond the $500 annual savings limit and eliminate the income ceiling to ensure that there are more resources in the system. McPherson responded that IRAs are the best part of the relief legislation, but not really strong. He believes that opening up existing IRAs for other uses is "unambiguously bad" from a U.S. savings point of view because people will deplete these savings, and opening up income ceilings won't help people to save because this will affect only people who have been saving already. McPherson suggested that we focus on IRAs where *new* money goes to help pay for education and on people who are not likely to save otherwise.

Walter Moulton, director of Student Aid at Bowdoin College, wondered if anyone has given thought to alumni giving as the landscape changes; what will alumni feel for a college as the sources of revenue change, and how inclined will they feel to help their alma mater? Schapiro replied that he is struck by how little we know about why people give, so it is hard to forecast what will happen in the future. The amount of revenue for higher education that comes from gifts and endowment earnings has been increasing at private and public institutions, and "we

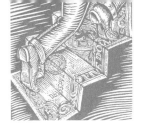

will be relying more upon the philanthropy of our alumni in the future." How will they feel now that they are paying more and graduating with larger debt burdens? Are they going to be as generous? Schapiro admitted he does not know the answer.

Joe Paul Case, dean of Financial Aid at Amherst College, asked about "upper income melt": what is their reaction to the idea that perhaps over time as college costs have increased beyond family incomes, the "pinch factor" for these families has increased and led them to send students to universities rather than high-priced colleges? Schapiro says this is a good explanation of what is happening, and not unlike what is happening in other product markets: the mid-level, reasonably-to-higher-priced products have suffered the most. People are moving to stable, middle-of-the-road, lesser-priced institutions or, if they are going to spend a lot for education, will only spend it at the name-brand institutions. McPherson added that he thinks another indirect effect of the high expense these days is more of a bottom-line mentality among families. Universities generally do a better job of showing where a degree from their institution will lead in terms of career than private liberal arts colleges have done, and they also get more corporate recruiters to their campuses. Small colleges need to take advantage of consortial arrangements and the corporate recruitment or career area would be a good one with which to start.

Bruce Poch, dean of Admissions at Pomona College, asked, "How much of the recent upper-income increase comes from the increase in two-career families?" Schapiro responded that the greatest increase in two-wage earner families actually took place in the 1970s because the economy was so bad that many families needed two incomes just to get by. While there was a higher percentage of two-income families in 1995 than in 1980, comparing the percentage of high-income families in 1970 with that of 1995 would show a greater difference.

Dr. Michael S. McPherson is a nationally known economist, writer, and authority on the financing of higher education. He has been a consultant on enrollment, tuition, and financial aid policy to liberal arts colleges and universities around the country and was a senior fellow at the Brookings Institution. He is the coauthor and editor of seven books, including, with Dr. Schapiro, *Keeping College Affordable: Government and Educational Opportunity* (1991) and *Paying the Piper: Productivity, Incentives, and Financing in Higher Education* (1993). Before coming to Macalester as president in 1996, McPherson served for twenty-two years at Williams College as professor, chair of the Economics Department, and dean of the faculty.

Dr. Morton Owen Schapiro is a widely quoted authority on college financing and affordability, and on trends in education costs and student aid. He is author or coauthor of dozens of articles and five books, including those mentioned above coauthored with Dr. McPherson. Dr. Schapiro has received numerous contracts and research grants from the National Science Foundation, the U.S. Department of Education, the World Bank, the Andrew W. Mellon Foundation, the Spencer Foundation, the College Board, and other agencies to study the economics of higher education and related topics. He is also a commentator on Public Radio International. Prior to becoming dean of the University of Southern California in 1994, Dr. Schapiro was chair of its Department of Economics.

College Affordability: How Are Institutions and Families Coping?

Rebecca Dixon, associate provost of University Enrollment at Northwestern University, served as panel moderator and described the panel's role as reacting to the main themes of the colloquium — cost and affordability — from their own perspectives. Dixon asked each panelist to share the key worries they have in relation to these issues.

Joellen Silberman, dean of Financial Aid and Enrollment at Kalamazoo College, led off with her concern about the sentiments that pervade our culture now: "Parents feel that someone else should pay for their child's education, that loads of aid has been talked about for the last fifteen years and 'where is mine?' and that college is the same as other consumer goods: no one should pay full price." Silberman also struggled with issues related to "competing as a private college with institutions that cost up to 50 percent less, or with name-brand institutions that have similar costs... We are different from other marketing environments in that our consumer is our product, and moving to appease consumers may compromise the product."

Bill Young, director of Enrollment Management at Colorado School of Mines, expressed concern about the growing complexity of the process and what one has to know to try to make things work in an equitable fashion. Beyond that, what worries him most is if and how senior management listens to middle managers. "Middle managers have insights that need to be considered, and need to get upper administration to think beyond a one-year perspective." Young finds it "increasingly difficult to meet an institution's larger goals in the face of concerns about the bottom line and our loss of control over the dynamics of the process."

Panelist Penny Sommers, college counselor at John C. Fremont High School, described her school as a large public high school, where 95 percent of the students are Latino, 5 percent are African

American, and 40 to 45 percent go on to college. She said, "I'm scared that we are closing doors to our first-generation students, our underrepresented students, and our poor students. We are limiting their access, not just in the application process itself, but by setting up invisible obstacles: reducing their belief that college is in their future." She is concerned that limiting their access and reducing their prospects will have a great impact on our society as a whole. Sommers finds the current aid policies very troubling from this perspective, as students who are qualified for college-level work — but without the high grades or scores that would ensure them the best proportion of grant to loan — have to take on more paid work to make ends meet, live off-campus, or attend school part-time, all of which may jeopardize their chances of academic success or of having a complete college experience.

Next, Sandy Baum, professor of Economics at Skidmore College, provided a two-part perspective: "As an economist, my primary concern is what is happening to access for lower-income students while we are worrying about affordability for the middle- and upper-income groups." She fears that college may come to reinforce the existing class structure rather than provide opportunities for upward mobility. "As a faculty member, I worry that all the pressure to keep costs down makes it hard to keep the real educational mission of an institution at the forefront."

Frank Campanella, executive vice president at Boston College, followed, saying "The things I worry about are exactly the same things I worried about in 1973": price and cost and their relationship at higher-education institutions. He considers "cost" as the cost of doing business; by "price," he means the tuition that is charged. Aid and admission are only part of the equation. "Education is both labor intensive and capital intensive," he said, and we are just starting to see any progress in becoming less labor intensive through the use of technology. He stressed that

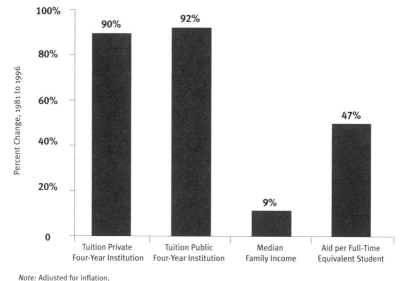

Note: Adjusted for inflation.
Source: Based on *Trends in Student Aid, 1987 to 1997*, Table 3 (The College Board, Washington, D.C: 1997) and NCES data.

Figure 1. 15-year changes in tuition, family income, and student aid.

"the solution isn't downsizing but rather to understand the work we do and eliminate work that is redundant, unnecessary, or too costly."

Larry Gladieux, executive director for Policy Analysis at the College Board, referred to the chart, *15-Year Changes in Tuition, Family Income, and Student Aid.* He pointed out that, over the past 15 years, in adjusted dollars, four-year public and private institution tuition has doubled, while family incomes have gone up 9 percent. Gladieux noted that this figure "masks" the real growth at the upper-income level, the stagnation at middle-income levels, and the decrease at the lowest income levels. Financial aid has gone up 47 percent. "I worry that it will look like this again from the perspective of the next 15 years — and we will have closed off lots of opportunities for underrepresented, low-income, and first-generation students: those with the most need and highest risk." Also, since Gladieux

was filling in on this panel for Bruno Manno, executive director of the National Commission on the Cost of Higher Education, he added that he believes the federal government does not have the leverage or the mandate to weigh in on the price and cost issue: only 10 percent of higher education revenue comes from the federal government.

The audience then had a chance to respond. Michael Behnke, vice president for Admissions and Financial Aid at the University of Chicago, wondered why more institutions have not followed Boston College's cost-cutting strategies. Campanella responded that it is really a lot of hard work. Boston College looked at the cost of everything that the college does except the instance where a faculty member goes into a class or lab to teach or do research (that was already done as part of an academic financing exercise). Just one part of the project is to look at these three areas: all the processes that affect students, all the processes that affect faculty and administrative support, and all the processes that affect the management of the physical plant. Another facet of the project is to look at the whole organizational structure from the top down.

Joyce Smith, executive director of the National Association of College Admissions Counselors (NACAC), asked the panelists what they see as the changes ahead for institutions in the next ten years as they try to cope with affordability issues. Bill Young responded, "When 40 to 90 percent of your students need financial assistance in order to pay for college, your cost structure is out of control." He thinks that in the face of this, super-competitive institutions will change little; public institutions may not change much either because they receive subsidies; high-priced institutions without prestige or subsidies will suffer if they don't come up with sharp aid-management solutions. Some colleges may adapt by serving the nontraditional marketplace. Joellen Silberman sees changes at

Kalamazoo already; downsizing has led to a more "Web-like" administrative structure, and the faculty is following the lead by considering nondiscipline-based departments. Baum concurred that there will be some sorting out. "In some cases, technology will help to translate some types of knowledge, but there will always be aspects of education that simply cannot be done that way," she said. Campanella added that it is not necessarily a cost saver to substitute technology for faculty teaching, but that it can save money on the administrative side. Dixon alluded to the fact that "we are all trying to keep up with the Joneses" in services ranging from counseling to security to campus shuttles; families think they need these services even if their students never use them, and at some point the range of services offered needs to be revisited.

Don Saleh asked Penny Sommers what counselors think of the situation where more merit aid is going to low-need, high-ability students. She replied that her greatest concern is whether these policies are communicated "proactively," so that parents and counselors can help students make intelligent college choices. Colleges need to level the playing field by providing solid information to everyone, not just to feeder high schools or to the types of students who already have greater access to college application information.

Frank Palmasani, counselor at Hinsdale South High School, wondered about moving the aid process up one year, so that students would get award letters at the end of their junior year, giving them more time to plan. Bill Young responded that we are "talking as if 18-year-olds are rational people. Maybe one year *later* would be better."

Judy Lewis-Logue, director of Financial Aid Services at the University of San Diego, commented that communicating these issues to high school students misses the opportunity for early outreach to students not yet in high school; these younger students

and families are still trusting in the system the way it used to be.

Barry Adams, vice president for Enrollment Management at Saint Mary's University, asked, "Can anyone tell a family how much a college will really cost for four years?" Young replied that a reasonable response can be given: we can extrapolate what tuition might be well into the future, and can make reasonable assumptions about aid options and what loan levels might be. Gladieux agreed with Adams that "there is a lot of confusion out there" and with Young that it should be possible to put some figures together that would help people plan.

Peter Latson, assistant director, Upper School at Hackley School, indicated that in the past, he saw "opportunities for students with low scores and low ability to pay," many of whom were students of color. Given the current situation with affirmative action, what do panelists see happening to this group? Sommers replied that "community colleges are still available, but only a few four-year colleges seem willing to take a chance" on these students anymore.

Nancy Beane, college counselor at The Westminster Schools, stated, "The [Georgia] Hope Scholarship is an entitlement for the middle class; the federal government doesn't care about the low-income family, and colleges don't want to use their own funds for high-need students. Who is expanding access for lower-income students?" Young conceded that while "options do exist for high-need, highly qualified students, access for high-need, less-qualified students is a struggle." As for the (Georgia) Hope Scholarships, "students who meet the B-average criteria tend to be from the middle-income group, but it was not designed as a middle-class benefit per se." Baum added that if you look at data, some low-scoring, high-need students are being admitted, indicating that "some colleges *are* looking beyond scores to see what else the students have to offer. But part of the social issue that we have a very hard time talking

about is the fact that the same type of education is not appropriate for everyone. For some of these students, a particular college is not the answer — there are other problems to be addressed that go beyond the financial aid questions."

Rebecca Dixon closed the session by cautioning, "We have to be careful about how we look to cut costs. If we backtrack on affirmative action, we will not be embodying the American vision. We have to be careful that our generation does not leave the legacy of education only for the wealthy."

Small Group Discussions on College Affordability and Enrollment Challenges

Participants broke into small groups to discuss the following questions.

1. How can colleges and universities convince families that the value derived from an undergraduate education today is worth the price? How can we measure "value"? How can we describe "value"? Is there a difference in how public and private institutions would approach this question?

Nancy Monnich, director of Admissions and coordinator of Financial Aid at Bryn Mawr College, and Natala Hart, director of Financial Aid at The Ohio State University, led the discussion groups dealing with these issues. Rebecca Dixon remarked, "Given the cost and financial commitment, we cannot assume a robust definition of value on the part of students and families... We need to constantly reinforce the value of education and communicate with those who raise the question on a variety of levels." Frank Campanella stated that "disciplined study in a rigorous curriculum creates academic value, and a student's personal development enhances and reinforces this value." He cautioned that we should take a broad approach to defining value and not just focus on careers and earnings projections. Bob Shorb, director of Student Aid and Family Finance at Skidmore College, agreed that money outcomes should be mentioned last, after such values as contribution to society, becoming a better person, having more choices in the future, etc., are mentioned.

Participants believe confusion exists in the definition of value among tangible benefits, intangible benefits, current value, and future value. Value itself is not the same at all institutions or even for all students within an institution; it must be explained in a multidimensional way. Joe Paul Case asked, "What will people pay for quality?" He has concluded that it depends on where people are coming from and what kind of background and

information they bring to the process; education is an intangible asset that is differently priced, and its value is a function of how families see it. Several participants indicated that there are two different perceptions of value: that of the family and that of the institution; the trick is to bring these together. To do so, the institutional definition of value should be clear, and communication is essential. The marketing effort should begin early on, and there is a role for the College Board in this effort. Institutions need to be clear about costs and borrowing and emphasize that it is important to save for college because it is worth saving for. Some participants felt that it would be important to extend the message to families that simply cannot save, given their financial situation, that they should consider academic support as their investment; they also acknowledged that it would be hard to "market" that line.

The majority of participants in these groups felt that any public or private differences on the issue of value were not significant. Dolan Evanovich, associate provost for Enrollment at the University of Connecticut, did feel there is a "different twist" for public institutions, which offer value in terms of the breadth of opportunity for the price that is paid.

2. What can colleges do to ensure an economically diverse student body, while at the same time controlling the discount rate or the financial aid budget? Is there a difference in how public and private institutions would approach this question?

Stephanie Balmer, director of Admissions at Agnes Scott College, and Joseph Merante, associate vice president for Academic Affairs at Loyola Marymount University, led the discussion groups on this topic. Bob Massa, dean for Enrollment Management at Johns Hopkins University, believes the commitment to diversity has to come first (with a commitment from upper management and not just from the

enrollment office) before an institution can find ways to fund the commitment. "For example, you might make those students exempt from a need-aware policy if one is in place." Other basic strategies participants suggested included being sure that, for low-income students, colleges have programs that help them comply with deadlines from state programs and take advantage of every outside source there might be.

Jerry Davis, vice president for Research at the Sallie Mae Education Institute, asked if anyone questions whether an economically diverse student body serves the institution; he thinks public and private colleges differ on this. Massa suggested that diverse students help complete the educational experience, and Merante said the question isn't should it be done but can it be done. Others said that economic diversity per se is not the mandate, but rather racial diversity. Terry Whitehill, assistant director of the Office of Admissions at Indiana University, said, "IU struggles with competition with other national public institutions that might be more attractive; we compete for in-state students because of the tuition subsidy — but this doesn't accomplish our ethnic diversity goals, because much of that pool is out of state." Other participants concluded that no one — the federal government, college presidents, faculty — mandates diversity anymore; there is a sense of "Who cares?"

As for controlling the discount rate, Massa said, "Price influences the discount rate. Controlling price by controlling costs will control the discount rate. There needs to be a top-down commitment to evaluating the costs and the need for services." Davis asked whether colleges might want to consider charging differential tuition based on program cost, or consider articulation agreements with other institutions to control costs. David Busse, director of Financial Aid at Macalester College, responded, "Colleges continue to charge what they can, to keep up with peer institutions." Myra Smith, director of Financial Aid

at Smith College, commented that colleges need to figure out the financial impact of the relationship between tuition and the discount. Others agreed, indicating that raising tuition may not lead to net revenue increases. And several participants indicated that articulation agreements (for transfer students) could help control costs and assure access; four-year institutions could bring in low-income students for their last two years and diversify the student body without having to absorb the cost for four years.

In terms of merit aid, Stuart Perry, associate director of Student Financial Services at Carleton College, said that the issue goes back to the applicant pool at each college; colleges respond to their individual pools. Abigail Parsons, associate vice president of Admission and Financial Aid at Pitzer College, said Pitzer offered some merit aid last year and had problems getting the desired mix of economic diversity. Merante asked, "How does a need-aware policy with merit aid control the discount rate and shape the class? Are financial aid people part of this discussion on their campuses?" Massa reiterated that these decisions all come back to the institution and its mission, priorities, and enrollment goals. John Brugel, director of Financial Aid at Rutgers University, noted, "Public institutions use merit aid as a defense against losing high-ability students." Participants discussed a number of public university merit aid programs, including ones in place or under consideration in Minnesota, New Jersey, New York, and Iowa; few of these serve low-income students, but a proposal in Massachusetts would target needy merit students.

3. **How can we reach out to the families of the lowest income, the most disadvantaged students, to assure them that college is not beyond their reach despite rising costs? When should we reach out to those families? What should government's role in this effort**

be? Institutions' role? Higher-education associations' role? Others' role?

Jim Miller, director of Financial Aid at Harvard and Radcliffe Colleges, Nancy Beane, college counselor at The Westminster Schools, and Lois Mazzuca, college counselor at Glenbrook North High School, led the groups discussing these topics.

Several participants acknowledged that colleges have never been successful in the outreach effort to these families; sending out glossy brochures and videos may well not be the most effective way to reach this group. But in some cases, colleges may have oversold the concept of universal choice and access; Jim Miller said that concept "may represent a brief moment in time." Pamela Johnson, associate dean and director of Financial Aid at College of Saint Catherine, acknowledges that her state's aid programs "assure *access* at public colleges for low-income disadvantaged students, but not *choice*." Bill Young indicated that high-ability, low-income students have no problem — there is great demand for them — but low-income, low-ability students don't have as many choices. "This is not just a question of money; we need to ask whether we are doing the right thing for these students by trying to find a way to enroll them." Peter Latson ventured, "Maybe open access is not the ideal. We already enroll more students in higher education than any other country in the world — maybe that's not right."

Beane summarized the impact of increasing college costs and the decreasing power of the Pell Grant, pointing out that in the 1970s the maximum Pell award covered three quarters of the average cost at public institutions and one third of average private college costs. In 1997, the maximum Pell award covered one third of public college costs and one seventh of private college costs. Mazzuca conceded, "We may not be able to assure them that college is not beyond their reach unless there is additional support from state and federal governments."

As for how and when to reach out to low-income, disadvantaged students, participants felt that it is important to consolidate the message. Arthur Doyle, vice president for Field Services and Corporate Marketing at the College Board, suggested using "the United Negro College Fund approach of one message rather than each institution attempting to reach out independently." Also, use the most effective media, and get the message out earlier than the traditional junior and senior years of high school. Bill Schilling, director of Student Financial Services at the University of Pennsylvania, said, "The key is to give enough assurance early on — fifth or sixth grade — that it changes behavior and students focus on their responsibility in achieving the goal of higher education." But participants agreed it is hard to get family attention at this stage, and difficult to hold their attention over a period of time; often this group is likely to respond to hearsay and rumor rather than formal information. Participants agreed the issue should be tackled vigorously at the state and local levels, perhaps by providing success stories rather than the annual headlines about college costs going up. David Strauss, principal of the Arts & Science Group, suggested that the government should coordinate the effort for early outreach, as it is in the best interest of the country's future taxpayers. Young responded, "Unfortunately, the government doesn't think ten years down the line."

Others suggested that colleges and corporations make connections with particular schools and work with middle and high school counselors and students to help students prepare for college, focusing energy on the youngest possible ages. Terry Jackson, director of Financial Aid at Knox College, described a program where Knox College, the local community college, and local high schools work together to "guarantee low-income, first-generation, high-ability eighth graders" access to two years at the community college and two years at Knox; Don Saleh said a similar program operates at Cornell. Others

indicated how important it is to provide mentoring and support
along the way so that students will qualify for aid when they
reach college. But Christopher Walsh, director of Financial Aid
at Syracuse University, acknowledged that all too often "there is
no shared responsibility... We at Syracuse can attract a low-
income, disadvantaged student to our door, but the money *really*
isn't there to cover educational costs."

**4. What can we do to help middle- and upper-income
families be better prepared to pay their share of
college costs? How do we reach families when their
children are very young to maximize their preparation
time? Will the provisions of the Taxpayer Relief Act
of 1997 encourage families to begin saving early? What
can the financial aid system do to encourage
and support planning and saving?**

Marcelle Tyburski, director of Student Aid at Colgate University,
Diane Stemper, director of Financial Aid at Miami University,
and John Curtice, assistant vice chancellor for Student Affairs
and Financial Aid at State University of New York, led the
discussion groups considering these questions. Many
participants agreed that a massive media effort is needed to get
the message out about saving for college and starting early.
Currently, the media is negative in that it is teaching families
how to bargain; Tyburski indicated that professionals in aid have
been "forced" to move away from the principles of need analysis,
and now need to move back to the fact that families do indeed
bear the primary burden of meeting college costs.

Laura Talbot, director of Financial Aid at Swarthmore College,
suggested that family attitudes about saving changed with the
Middle Income Student Assistance Act in 1978. Nancy McDuff,
director of Admission at the University of Georgia, surmised that
it is a generational problem: current parents are still paying for
their own education and haven't saved. George Mills, vice

president for Enrollment at the University of Puget Sound, said, "Families are not prioritizing education in their savings... they believe they can pay for college through current income, and upper-income families see equal value at public schools as at private ones." Families need to be made aware that the financial aid system is not there to support families with incomes that would indicate they have had the capacity to save through the years. Jim Belvin, director of Financial Aid at Duke University, is convinced we need "radical, different, new ideas" that match family lifestyles today to encourage saving, such as new types of college savings programs as part of employee benefit packages. Ed Below, director of Financial Aid at Wesleyan University, spoke of the new state prepaid tuition plans being problematic in that they are not standard state to state, and they raise issues for public versus private institutions; perhaps "portability" could be encouraged.

As for the Taxpayer Relief Act of 1997, Belvin indicated that it will be difficult from an administrative perspective. It is likely to shut down future appropriations for aid; and, while it may change consumer spending patterns, it will not necessarily mean more money for college. Below suggested that education tax credits may lead to "increased awareness" in the same way that energy tax credits did in the past. Others suggested the act probably will not encourage new savings — but is good anyway in terms of focusing attention on ways to pay for college.

Most participants agreed that a better job of encouraging savings needs to be done, and that FASSAC is working on this. Among messages suggested was this from Bob Donaghey, director of Financial Aid at Middlebury College: "By saving, parents are taking back the ability to decide where their child goes to college." Others suggested the importance of emphasizing that it is better to earn interest than to pay it — focus on saving early rather than borrowing later. The "pay over

time" concept (before, during, after college) needs to be communicated more broadly. Some wondered, "Are families paralyzed when it comes to saving for college, or are they just indifferent?" Some suggested that there is "little truth" to the fact that savings are a disincentive in need analysis; families don't realize what a small percentage of these savings are tapped by colleges. There was general agreement that disclosure of an institution's aid practices — as well as what costs are and why — is crucial to allowing families to plan ahead.

5. **What can colleges do to maintain or increase the quality of their student body, while ensuring access through their need-based aid programs? What should be the role of government in encouraging academic achievement?**

Scott Healy, director of Undergraduate Admissions at Ohio State University, and Joseph Allen, vice provost for Enrollment and dean of Admission and Financial Aid at the University of Southern California, led the two small groups discussing this question. As for maintaining or increasing the quality of the student body while ensuring access through need-based programs, some participants focused on what it is we would maintain access to. John Baworowsky, vice president for Admission and Financial Aid at North Park University, said, "We are lacking respect for the technical trades; we need a system to permit students to choose such an option and have it be well regarded." Nancy Meislahn, director of Admissions at Cornell University, extended that remark by reiterating that the diversification of institutions is important. "We need to resist the temptation to keep up with the Joneses and rather focus on who the right students are for our institution. Are all institutions right for all students?"

Todd Hutton, vice president of Academic Administration at Willamette University, remarked that managing aid is a science and relies on both cost containment and knowing and working

within your institution's niche. Steve Brooks, executive director of the North Carolina State Education Assistance Authority and College Board Trustee, added, "An institution's position and resources will influence what it is able to do." One participant noted that public institutions are in a different situation than private ones: the family median income is lower at private colleges than at public ones; tuition could be raised significantly at public institutions and not affect the quality of the student body.

Julia Perreault, director of Financial Aid at Emory University, remarked that there has been a blurring of the distinction between need and merit aid; students feel if they are admitted they are entitled to scholarship aid. Many participants indicated that developing a better social contract with parents and families is essential. Perreault feels that we need to turn the talk from the discount rate to the value of the education itself; merit scholarships may work in the short run but could compromise the social contract. Jim Swanson, director of Financial Aid at Colorado College, said that "the question assumes that needy students are not academically talented, but there are many academically talented needy students. Perhaps we could design capital campaign strategies to target a merit component within need-based aid." He fears we are "backing into merit aid because of fund-raising considerations rather than philosophy." There was an acknowledgment that merit scholarships are a part of the mix and that they are used to promote quality; there was not as much agreement that they are necessarily used at the expense of need-based aid. Other participants suggested that merit aid is a "quick fix," and that perhaps special academic programs should be developed to attract high-quality students, rather than depending on merit aid. Many participants also expressed concern over the debt levels students are assuming.

As for government's role, most participants would like to see it more limited in scope and focused not on merit but on need.

Perreault shared with the group that the Hope Scholarships in Georgia led to grade inflation at the high school level and put pressure on college professors to award grades to ensure scholarship renewal; "merit aid should be institution-specific," she said. Perreault acknowledged that it is a nightmare to monitor state and federal programs on a large scale; in Georgia, about half of Hope Scholars lose the scholarship in the second year, and then institutions have to scramble to find money for those with need. Barbara Tornow, executive director of the Office of Financial Assistance at Boston University, suggested that the role of the government should be in encouraging persistence: awarding super grants to institutions based on their ability to graduate students. Jim Scannell, president of Scannell and Kurz, Inc., cautioned that any standard measure of achievement would have to take into consideration the differences among student bodies served by various institutions; those enrolling large numbers of low-income students should not be discriminated against. Barowowsky agreed that you can't change the profile of the student body dramatically; institutions could measure where they are today and use that as the baseline to measure improvement. "The College Board needs to rally the troops, not just within the government but in the public at large to support need-based grants," he said. Arnaldo Rodriquez, vice president for Admission and Financial Aid at Pitzer College, felt the government should be involved only in establishing minimum admission requirements for public institutions.

What Are the Cost Drivers? What Can We Do About Them? What Can We Say About Them?

Katharine Hanson, president of the Consortium on Financing Higher Education (COFHE), moderated this panel charged with exploring issues surrounding college costs. She indicated that the panelists would explore (1) what the cost drivers are, (2) differences between cost and price and between public and private institutions on these issues, and (3) how we explain costs to families.

Jay Morley, president of the National Association of College and University Business Officers (NACUBO), started the panel discussion by saying that he sees the current economy in general as having moved from producer driven to consumer driven. Just as health care has been affected by this new economy, so has education: we have moved from the producers (faculty)driving higher education to consumers (parents, students, and policymakers) as the drivers of the process. Morley emphasized that this change in the marketplace should motivate colleges and universities to think strategically about costs.

Morley then shared with the group the cost drivers he has identified:

1. **Faculty to student ratio:** "As long as we think of the 1:15 faculty to student ratio as immutable, we won't go anyplace with reducing costs." Costs are driven by how much it costs to do what we do, he said, and only 20 percent of an institution's budget is on the administrative side; the rest is faculty costs. "Chipping away at the administration will get you some savings, but it won't solve the problem."

2. **Faculty and facility costs:** Colleges and universities have worked within "a fixed enrollment size." Education does not have the opportunities that other businesses do to spread costs around as they go up. Costs for faculty and facilities have gone up about 4 to 5 percent a year, while tuition has generally gone up 2 to 3 percent annually to help meet those costs.

3. **Cross-subsidies:** Morley acknowledged that most institutions have not sorted out well just where these are. He shared a general parameter: "About 80 percent of credit hours are taught in 20 percent or fewer of the courses listed in a college's catalog." Morley alluded to the University of Phoenix, which deals in a competitive market and has responded well to it, focusing on that 80 percent.

4. **Indirect cost recovery:** At research universities, a major cost driver is reduced indirect cost recovery. The total pool of research dollars has lost $10 million to $20 million, as the government has drastically reduced reimbursement of overhead for research. Morley does not expect these funds to return.

5. **Technology:** We do not yet have the payback in increased efficiency to match the investment in technology, he said.

6. **Institutional financial aid:** Morley conceded that NACUBO may well have been the organization to coin the term *tuition discounting* but will stop using that term and get back to *institutional aid* to "help get the term off the radar screen."

7. **Facilities:** A NACUBO study indicated that $20 billion to $30 billion is needed across the country for the backlog in "really critical maintenance" to get facilities into shape. Savings can be depleted millions at a time by upkeep projects.

8. **Rising expectations:** "Now that tuition is so high, people think they deserve more in terms of services," Morley said.

Next, Michael McPherson spoke about cost versus price. He believes that in this consumer-driven economy, consumers "don't care about *cost*, but do care a lot about what they have to *pay* for education; parents don't really care about hidden costs." He emphasized that 80 percent of all paying customers have their children in public institutions, where prices have gone up a

lot in percentage terms over the past eight to ten years. This makes for the energy that is attached to this issue. There is more political attention paid to the cost issue now — even though the dramatic private college real price increases ended about five years ago — because of what has been going on in the public sector. "And on that side, it is not a cost issue at all; rates of growth in real costs to students have been very low, under 1 percent a year. What's out of control is not costs, but the reduced willingness of state legislatures to continue funding higher education," he said.

From the mid-1980s to the mid-1990s, states withdrew $7 billion to $10 billion in annual support to higher education. The Taxpayer Relief Act of 1997 will provide $7 billion to $10 billion annually. McPherson terms this "a reverse federalism." "The political battle is largely driven by these shifts in funding for higher education, and not by serious thinking about what it costs to produce education. Even on the private college side, the bottom line has been about endowment; the bottom line in a 1997 article in *Time* was about Penn's subsidy from its endowment, especially who was going to get these monies, this generation or future ones.

"Cost control at public institutions has been remarkably effective — because there haven't been any dollars there," he said. Institutions have implemented early retirement programs, increased class size, reduced course choices, and done less hiring. The institutions themselves are not sure if these have been the most effective ways to cut costs. McPherson shared with the group a belief of Bruce Johnstone, chancellor at State University of New York at a time of cost cutting, that these measures are far from efficient, but have more to do with dealing with a state body to plan an institution's budget. "If you make intelligent plans for *future* cuts, those cuts tend to be made *immediately* by the legislature."

Moving from the cost versus price issue to the issue of underlying costs, McPherson asked, "Where could you look to deliver a high-quality education while cutting costs?" McPherson is convinced we need "a more searching examination of the nature and the measurement of and the reward for faculty work. Our current crude definition, showing up for a certain number of classes, does not help us get at the essentials. We need a more articulate, richer definition of what we hope our faculty will accomplish as a starting point for moving toward making education more effective."

Next, Thomas Rajala, director of Admission at Boston University, tackled the topic "How do we talk about affordability and costs?" Rajala is concerned about the increased tendency to talk about education in terms of costs. For example, a 1:15 faculty to student ratio strikes economists as limiting from a financial point of view, whereas it represents what Rajala and many students and parents *want* to see. Students should ask "Who will teach me?" and we will need to provide a good answer, he said.

As admission and financial aid administrators," Rajala continued, "we are charged to go out there and help people understand who we are and what we are and why we are as institutions. A frustration is that while we are rarely invited to conversations about the cost drivers — new dining plans, faculty: student ratios, new athletic centers — we are constantly expected to be able to effectively present the benefits of these attributes to families as they work to address how they will pay for college."

He also warned that we should be careful about the terms we use. "Terms like *sticker price*, once used only for cars, undermine the real value of education... Automobiles depreciate the minute they leave the lot — while education is one of the few things we acquire that will never lose value... It will *gain* value as we go along." Rajala then referred to the term *discounting*. "This was

never put forth by financial aid and admission officers as a formal strategy or solution." Rather, as we ran into enrollment problems, we took a series of incremental steps in providing financial assistance, taking into account a family's willingness to pay, that led toward what we now all accept as practices covered by the term *discounting*, he said.

Rajala shared with the group that he recently received a letter from a middle schooler, written as part of a class project. In addition to other questions about BU, the student asked, "What do you do with the tuition that we pay?" Rajala suggested that we all need to "think carefully about how we describe what we offer and the costs associated with it, and the more we can talk about education in terms of investment rather than expenditure, the better off we will be, as this question underlies much of our interaction with families."

He urged the group to focus on the attributes, value, and results of the investment. "Education should produce a condition of lifelong curiosity." One unique aspect of education is "you can customize your education at no additional cost" by adding art exhibits, concerts, guest lectures, or pursuing interdisciplinary or double majors. In conclusion, Rajala stated, "Other things we purchase can or must be replaced. But there is no replacement for the initial undergraduate experience; this is a suggestion of value families may not have considered and which we should point out to them."

In response to other panelists, McPherson said, "What Thomas [Rajala] said about education was wonderful. But finding another term for discounting may not be what we need to do. If we are uneasy about the behavior behind the term, then we should change the behavior." Morley said we need to engage the faculty and administration in the understanding of financial issues: "Financial officers *do* believe in education — but the cost issues are where we are getting hammered. We can confess we

41

have a cost problem — what we do *is* expensive — but we can look for cost solutions, not just focus on value to deflect criticism." Katharine Hanson shared with the group that she thinks the current cost commission will be seen as a failure and that the cost issue won't go away. "Congress and the media will continue to say we have a cost problem and won't do anything about it ourselves — so 'someone else' will have to do something about it." Hanson outlined the various topics within the commission's discussion — controlling costs, deregulation, colleges sharing responsibility on the cost issue, providing information to the public about what college will cost (financial transparency), and responding to concerns and misunderstandings about how families can afford college. Morley remarked that the "irony is that the institutions most likely to be able to have an impact on resolving these issues are very unlikely to take up the invitation — given the recent antitrust litigation."

The panel was then opened up for audience response. Rebecca Dixon asked, "Where should we be in five to ten years to have resolved this controversy? Should we lower costs? Use better explanations? Admit more middle-income students?" Morley said we have to make changes that are obvious; the industrial sector also criticizes education: they feel they have used technology to reduce costs, and we haven't. He also urged the group to persevere: "The last thing this country needs is to have liberal arts education decimated as we respond to these pressures." Hanson interjected that "most people have no idea how colleges spend the money they have, and we need to get the message out," and Morley warned that we should launch our own media effort "because others will speak for us if we don't." Hanson also thinks we will begin in the next ten to fifteen years to reap the benefits of cost-cutting measures implemented in the 1990s, as well as see benefits from technology, particularly as new faculty and students will increasingly have

expertise and interest in making the technology work as an educational tool.

Joe Paul Case concurred that we can reexamine how teaching is done, use technology, etc. "But I'm also reminded of the recent *Doonesbury* cartoon with Ph.D.s looking for part-time jobs. What does the growth in part-time faculty do to the quality of education? To academic freedom?" McPherson responded that "academic freedom penetrates deeply into the organization of traditional colleges. We take 32 bits of knowledge and assign each to one producer to form an undergraduate education, and each faculty member is essentially a loner. This is the outcome of the genuine value to ensure faculty autonomy — but it is a real impediment to innovation in how to deliver education differently." As for part-timers: the University of Phoenix "gets part-time faculty as moonlighters from our types of institutions — they pick off the high-value, low-cost part of the market just as FedEx® picks off that part of the market from the U.S. Postal Service."

David Strauss commented, "There is a lot we could do together, especially in terms of getting parents involved in saving and the like — yet we are headed into intensified competition. Institutions will have to differentiate themselves more. The ugly reality is that we will be more likely to see haves and have-nots, especially among the private colleges."

John Lawlor, president of The Lawlor Group, Inc., followed up on the car references. "Sixty percent of luxury automobiles ($30,000-plus) are leased, not purchased. It's a question of cash flow: we are not savers but spenders." Most families don't have the cash flow to pay for college; how can we work to spread out costs? McPherson responded that there has been a lot of innovation in paying for college, including growth of parent loan programs. Hanson concurred that there has been a lot of innovation in the 1990s in terms of paying for college, but there

is a limit to the amount of debt you can take on, especially in some fields. National data on debt shows that it is going up substantially, and it is likely that debt will change what people do. Students who now take out a "30-year mortgage" on their own education will find it difficult to save for their children's education, or be philanthropic. So while institutions have created plans, the bottom line is people have to decide whether it is an investment worth saving for. What's happening now is that 80 percent of families are paying for part-time education spread over five to seven years; the minority of families are paying for four-year, full-time education.

Patricia Coye, director of Financial Aid at Pomona College, reminded the group that dropping costs would only help the folks at the top of the pool, who are the only ones who could pay the full amount — this wouldn't affect the rest of the student population. We need to create "more grant money to reduce debt levels for the true middle group," she said. Morley concluded, "We have to win the media battle. At the national policy level, a major issue is transfer of national wealth to the over-60 group; this group does not want to see cutbacks on Medicare, or their income taxed, to help educate the younger generation."

Helping Families Prepare to Pay for College: New Approaches for the 21st Century

Colloquium participants then had the chance to listen to views expressed by a panel moderated by Edwin Below, director of Financial Aid at Wesleyan University, and FASSAC chair. He indicated that the panel would focus on specific solutions to help families prepare to cover college costs.

"One of the most critical challenges we face is how to create incentives for people to save for college while their children are young," he said. College is the second- or third-largest investment a family will make, and requires financial planning. "Yet many expect that they will pay from current income or qualify for significant amounts of aid." The latter are the families that are often "angry or frustrated with the system and see us as denying their child a college education, at least where their child wants want to go."

Below reminded the group that, about ten years ago the CSS Committee on Standards of Ability to Pay (CSAP) advanced a concept, Sustained Annual Family Financial Effort (SAFFE) for paying for college over a number of years: precollege (saving); in college (current income); and postcollege (loans). The excuse families give for not saving in advance is the perceived disincentive in the need-analysis formula; Below believes it is more likely that parents "don't think about saving when their children are born, so then advance this excuse for not having saved once their children are ready for college…We in the aid profession know that the family that saves more has more options."

Below related that the work of FASSAC now is to create an incentive for saving. In discussions, the group has arrived at a new concept to make college payment as painless as possible, setting a goal of saving one third of the cost of college (based on the SAFFE premise), which can be accomplished most easily if families start early. An allowance for saving from current income would be included for younger siblings while older ones

are in college. In addition, assets accumulated as educational savings would be protected from the formula. Another option FASSAC is considering is to change the IM asset treatment by assessing all family assets (including those of the student) at the lower parents' rate. Below acknowledged this would have "a major impact on aggregate need since the proposal would reduce family contributions." He indicated that FASSAC is currently studying simulations of the impact of these proposals on a sample group of CSS/Financial Aid PROFILE® filers, and will refine and discuss the changes with the hope to implement a new strategy within the next several years. Below urged, "We need to make a greater effort to get people to save earlier," since paying for college is manageable if done that way.

As for the Taxpayer Relief Act of 1997, there will be a greater need to look at the IM and how it is impacted by and interacts with tax incentives. Below referred to the chart *Projecting a New Student Aid Environment*, which indicates that — once the tuition tax benefits are fully phased in — only 18 percent of the financial aid money in higher education will be awarded at the discretion of the individual colleges.

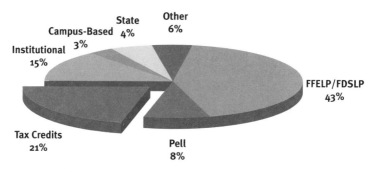

Note: Assumes $15 billion in tax cuts, when fully implemented in '96 dollars.

Sources: Based on *Trends in Student Aid, 1987 to 1997* (The College Board, Washington, D.C.: 1997) and estimates by the Washington Office of the College Board.

Figure 2. Projecting a new student aid environment: $15 billion in tax credits.

Thus, IM will influence the allocation of less money than in the past. Below remarked, "The impact of the IM formula will, in a sense, become diminished simply because it will influence less money that is distributed."

Shirley Ort, associate vice chancellor and director of Scholarships and Financial Aid at the University of North Carolina, Chapel Hill, spoke next about the states' role in helping families prepare through state-sponsored savings and tuition prepayment plans. She reminded the group of the subsidies provided to families in the pricing of public higher education; loans and credit financing are changing; tax policy is "the new thing on the horizon." Other nontraditional ways of paying for college include state-sponsored tuition prepayment programs and specially targeted funds for qualified students (such as state funding for workforce education or federal vocational education funding). "In sum, there are many methods of helping students and families from a wide array of incomes to pay for college, not all through Title IV."

Ort then focused on savings plans implemented by states, which fall into three types.

1. **Prepaid Tuition Plans:** following the development of prepaid tuition plans by a number of individual colleges in 1987, these types of state plans began in Michigan in 1989. In 1996, Congress passed a law clarifying tax status; such plans are now available in 14 states (eight just since 1996). "Lots more activity in this area can be expected."

2. **Savings Trust Programs:** in six states, these programs create the incentive to open a savings account and contribute on a regular basis to save for higher education.

3. **Zero-Coupon Bond:** college savings bonds, available in three states.

"In other words, about 24 states have one or more educational funding plans in place, and all but three states currently are engaged in research study or are considering legislation. At the state level, just about everyone will be engaged in these types of plans. We need to be prepared to deal with these," she said.

Ort then described three of the plans in more detail. In Florida, the program fully established in 1989 allows families to prepay tuition and residence hall charges risk free (the savings are backed by the state). There are three plans: for a baccalaureate at a four-year state college; for two years at a community college; or for two years at community college plus two years at a four-year state college. The average monthly contribution is $53, and the average household income for those who have chosen to participate is $50,000. About 376,000 contracts have been sold. The Ohio plan, authorized in 1989 and also backed by the state, sells units rather than credits; 100 units equal one year at a four-year baccalaureate institution. There are various options for payments. About 50,000 contracts have been sold. The Kentucky plan guarantees minimum earnings of 4 percent; deposits as small as $25 are accepted. The plan is for students currently 15 years old or younger. The savings are excluded from state student aid program eligibility. About 2,500 contacts have been sold. These plans have tried to make saving more affordable for low-income families. A major positive feature of prepaid tuition plans is that families can buy tomorrow's tuition at today's costs.

Sandy Baum spoke next, focusing on saving and borrowing as approaches for families to prepare to pay for college. She acknowledged, "The first step is to create a willingness to pay by making it clear what the value of the investment is, and what we do with the money they pay."

Why don't people save? In part, because "it is not a *perceived* savings disincentive — it *is* a disincentive." Baum agrees that we

need to let families know that they are better off if they save — but we also have to acknowledge the problems. Obviously, 5.6 percent is a low percentage to be taken of savings: there must be an exaggerated perception of what will be taken. Some economists say national savings have been discouraged by the savings disincentive in the need-analysis system. Baum is not convinced that national savings levels have been dramatically impacted by lack of saving for college. "But the more children you have, if you do amass major savings and will have children in college over eight to twelve years, your savings *will* be impacted dramatically."

Baum continued, "If we look at other disincentives in the need analysis system, we should look at what happens to the second income earner in the aid process. There's a disincentive to have a spouse work when children are in college because family income will be assessed at a higher rate. So many choose not to work when children are in college, which is outrageous on the face of it… It's not because people are *bad* that they react to these kinds of disincentives." Baum believes we have to acknowledge that that tension is there; downplaying the tax on assets can cut both ways.

"Incentives are created any time you treat assets differently." If families save money for college in vehicles created for that purpose and colleges don't assess those savings, but other people "saved in other savings vehicles with the same intention and are then considered to have an asset that the other families don't have, it's not only not fair but it creates the incentive for people to put their money in the places that are taxed less… If we can treat assets *less* differently — as Ed Below suggested with parent/student savings — that kind of fix makes the system less intrusive into people's behaviors." Baum also mentioned that there is an incentive built into the analysis for multiple children in college; it is to a family's advantage to "send the older one to Europe for a while" until the younger one is

ready to start. That is obviously not the intention of the policy, but it can lead to this type of family decision. Families will change behavior in response to what we do: "This is frustrating, but it is the reality."

Baum conceded that, even if all these problems were solved, most people would still have to borrow. "We fight against ourselves on this. Yes, college is an investment and it makes sense to borrow, but at the same time, it does fuel the panic on student-debt levels. Providing cautious advice on borrowing can make people think twice about borrowing. We need to focus on why it makes sense to borrow." Baum pointed out that the one third, one third, one third SAFFE concept often overlooks who pays. It is saying that parents can save and students can borrow (current income and savings come from parents but loans are generally taken by the students).

Baum indicated that the Sallie Mae student loan survey found no particular evidence that people are in trouble over the extent of borrowing. While the mean total college borrowing was $18,800, the median total debt was $13,000; there are a small number of people who borrow a lot of money (mainly law students) and pull the mean up. Also, these figures are for graduate and under-graduate school combined: for undergraduates, the median debt level was under $10,000. The students overwhelmingly said it was worth it for the investment. On the other hand, 40 percent said they had delayed buying a house, and a smaller percentage said they had delayed buying a car. "But their perceptions and reality do not mesh — there really was no impact on whether they bought a home, in part because their monthly student loan payments are very low versus what a house would cost." Baum said that, of the total that students owe after they graduate, about $150 a month goes to student loan repayment and a median of $700 a month goes to repay other types of loans. "This is not a paying-for-education problem: they want to go out after

college and live as if they had never paid for college... We need to help people think constructively about borrowing."

The audience then had a chance to respond. Joe Russo asked, "What about the student loan industry and the sometimes overly aggressive marketing of loans, as well as the marketing of credit cards to freshmen?" Baum responded that 25 percent of the students in the Sallie Mae survey had used credit cards "as a way to pay for college; this is a huge problem." As for student loan marketing, Baum acknowledged that the problem is there, but "I am concerned about a proposed solution to limit the availability of loans," since students need access to the liquidity. She agreed that borrowing responsibly is difficult to convey — it must be done by aid officers on an individual basis. Below added that much of the borrowing for education is beyond what is required for financing an education — much of it is discretionary, to enhance family lifestyle while children are in college. Ort added that she is concerned by the debt taken on by low-income students. In Washington State, a recent policy study found that at four-year public colleges, 83 percent of all aid award recipients were borrowing, with those in the lowest income group ($11,000 and below), taking on a $5,260 median loan in 1994-95.

Saleh commented that perhaps some of the difference in savings rates these days (9 percent 50 years ago versus 3 percent now) reflects that people 50 years ago saved for retirement, whereas they rely on corporate retirement plans now; it is likely those corporate savings plans are not considered in the 3 percent savings figure. Ort responded that the savings rate has declined even over the more recent years (from 5.5 percent in 1996 to the current 3 percent). Saleh also commented that treating student assets in the same manner as parent assets may make sense, because most student assets come from parents (or, as another participant noted, from grandparents). Below reiterated that the 35 percent assessment rate on student

savings "really is a problem." We encourage families to save in children's names for tax purposes and then penalize the savings in the need-analysis system. "But if we completely eliminated the 35 percent assessment rate, it would have tremendous impact on aggregate family contribution in the IM…we need to be careful, and we need more feedback."

Frank Palmasani alluded to development of retirement plans years ago through federal and corporate partnerships and said that if we really want to have people save more and take more ownership, we need to build tax incentives at the federal level as the Taxpayer Relief Act of 1997 has started to do. He added that colleges need to be very conscious of the disincentives they might create when families act on these. Below brought up the comment from one of the small group discussions, that we should encourage employers to participate with employees to set up savings programs or match savings or both; it is to their benefit to have an educated workforce.

David Strauss stated, "Admonishing people to save more is a naive approach to actually getting them to do it. The current evidence is that colleges are less and less likely to penalize children of non-savers if they want them on campus. Reducing *disincentives* probably won't dramatically change behavior. We need to come up with new *incentives* that have real benefits to families." Baum responded that dramatic new vehicles do make an impact on savings; payroll withholding for education savings would be a good idea because it can be seen as dramatic. Steve Brooks followed up by describing an education savings plan being developed in North Carolina, where parents will be allowed to accrue savings tax free, and have those savings taxed at the student's rate when used. The response to an early announcement of the outline of the program "has been tremendous and may serve as an example of the type of new incentive that can be effective."

Phil Wick, director of Financial Aid at Williams College, said, "We really don't know the limit of the amount of debt students can reasonably take on depending on their major field, especially in the face of the commercial loans that are proliferating... Is there any study of this being done?" Below conceded that students don't really know what they are going to do in terms of career until after college. Joe Merante indicated that at Loyola they are involved in a ten-year strategic plan and have tried to assess indebtedness to see which majors could assume higher debt levels. Humanities and social sciences faculty rebelled against the study, believing that education is not a career opportunity but a learning opportunity. Baum acknowledged that it is very difficult at the undergraduate level to tell what humanities majors will ultimately do, and suggested it is better to stick to averages when advising families.

Walter Moulton asked: "If we say, 'Save for college, and we won't count it in the need analysis,' and the beneficiary has a need, who ultimately pays? The federal and state governments won't, so will it be up to the college?" He also wondered how many states with savings plans have loan plans — a link between savings plans and loan plans would be a good incentive for families. Ort said she doesn't know if any of the plans are doing this.

Steven Thorndill, director of Financial Aid at the University of Puget Sound, wondered what would happen given that the IM savings disincentive may be a major factor in lack of savings nationally, what would happen if assets were ignored. Would people save more money if they thought they would not have assets "taken away" in the process? Baum commented that she is not convinced the financial aid system accounts for lower national savings, and that "ignoring assets is inequitable. Yes, we have to protect savings enough that people will put some money away. But totally ignoring assets would be totally unfair."

Wrap-Up and Next Steps

Wrap-Up

At the conclusion of the colloquium, Steven E. Brooks, executive director at the North Carolina State Education Assistance Authority, and College Board Trustee, presented a summary capturing the content and flavor of the discussions that had been held over the course of the two days. He began by indicating that Morton Schapiro and Michael McPherson had set the stage by providing a long view of revenue sources for higher education, and "alerted us to the fact that those sources were much the same in 1939-40" as they are in the 1990s. "Our keynoters asked the question, 'Are needy students paying more now than in the recent past?' and the answer is yes." Schapiro indicated that reported gains in median income mask the fact that the rich are richer and the poor are poorer. He also pointed out to us the "growing gap by race and income level in terms of college acceptance," and that there has been a real "melt" of 3 percent among the lowest-income students' college attendance. Brooks remarked, "The middle-income group has not been lost at private colleges, but upper-income families have moved increasingly to the elite private universities or to public universities."

McPherson shared with us an analysis for an imaginary university that moved to a targeted, need-aware financial aid strategy. He pointed out that this type of strategy can indeed cut costs in the financial aid budget, but that there are other costs associated with need-aware and merit policies. Differential packaging can be a source of confusion for families and represent the dilution of the "social contract" between colleges and families. Brooks seconded McPherson's caution: "It is important to be honest about the policies you do have — and be sure that your policies can bear the light of day." In an aside, Brooks referred to the issue of disclosure, which was a topic at last year's colloquium, and told the participants that the CSS Disclosure Work Group has been meeting and making progress

on this issue. Brooks then reminded the group of McPherson's conclusion that institutions and the government have a responsibility to maintain a need-based financial aid system — but the current political pressures and resulting tax credits illustrate the bad shape that need analysis is in. "Schapiro and McPherson left us with the question: Can we recover our framework of principles or, if not, create a new one?"

Brooks then gave a quick summary of the panel on college affordability and how institutions and families are coping (which Brooks subtitled "Experiential Angst: What Keeps Us Up at Night?"). He indicated that the concerns shared by the panel included the sense of entitlement among families today; the "growing complexity of our business and how to maintain equity in a complex process"; and the sense that we are closing the doors to poor and first-generation students. The panel also expressed concern about the focus on cost control to the detriment of educational quality, and the transfer of societal concern from access to affordability. The panel contends that we need to change the way we do business or we may face the same situation 15 years from now. "But if we cut costs willy-nilly, we may be in the position of knowing the cost of everything and the value of nothing." The panel concluded that there will be some sorting out of institutions that do not have the resources to meet the competition.

Brooks moved on to remind the group of the issues surrounding cost drivers that had been brought up by that panel. "We have moved from a producer-driven to a consumer-driven environment, and we need to recognize that the consumers are not just students and families but policymakers as well." He referred to the helpful list of cost drivers provided by Jay Morley, "to which you can add others for your own particular institution." Brooks then reminded the group of the distinction between cost and price that was made by

McPherson. McPherson pointed out that public costs have not so much risen recently, but rather state subsidies have declined. The affordability issue that has been raised has focused on the high-cost private institutions, where costs have not risen as much in recent years. "Another interesting comment about public institutions was that it's very difficult for them to plan to cut costs effectively, because if they do plan they tend to get zapped at the next session of the legislature." Brooks reminded the group that Rajala cautioned "we need to be careful how we articulate these cost issues, that we are not offering a product that depreciates, but providing an appreciating investment — and that we are also different in that students can customize their education at no extra cost." We need to be aware that families and policymakers want to know, "What do you do with the tuition we pay?" and we need to have answers for this. "We then heard a bit of a rebuttal; terminology is not really the issue…the issue is the behavior. The 'let's make a deal' mentality is what we may deplore more than the terminology." And we need to engage the faculty in these debates about costs, and let them be part of the solution. "We were reminded that the cost problem is not going to go away."

As for how we can help families prepare, Brooks said participants can "promote the concept that there are three ways families should be preparing to pay for college: before, during, and after the college years. And we can amend the methodology to minimize disincentives and offer incentives for saving." He reminded the group of the various ways states help families prepare: through state subsidies to public institutions, appropriations to student aid programs, tuition prepayment and savings programs, and workforce development programs, as well as savings initiatives. "We need to be aware that the states will be involved in the aid process: and that there will be at least 50 different implications for need analysis." There are some economists who think the disincentive for savings in need

analysis has had a dramatic impact on national savings levels. "I find that hard to believe, given the level of intelligent discourse I have had with families over the years — I just don't think they know a great deal about it — but it may have some impact on the margins." Brooks urged the group to think hard about treating different kinds of assets — such as state savings and Education IRAs — differently. The panelists provided information to indicate that there is no need for general panic on the issue of borrowing and debt levels. Finally, the discussion pointed out that there is an intergenerational transfer of payment obligations from parents to students: "Boomers are not paying for their children's education because they themselves didn't have to pay when they went to college."

Next Steps

Brooks then outlined for the participants some of the next steps for students and families, and the counselors who work with them, institutions, the government, and the College Board that emerged from colloquium discussions.

As for students and families, next steps would be:

- students should concentrate on academic achievement, especially if they have high need
- middle- and upper-income families should save more than they currently do
- families should demand disclosure of policies and practices (and we as professionals in enrollment need to provide answers to the questions students ask)
- students need to think carefully about the use of credit cards to finance college

For institutions, some next steps would be:

- think carefully about practices in light of mission, niche

in marketplace, and resources

- be mindful of the social contract and do the right thing to the extent possible
- develop partnerships with corporations and agencies; provide mentoring opportunities
- be aware of the demand for disclosure and be willing to disclose what we do; don't implement policies that won't bear the light of day
- reaffirm a commitment to need-based principles
- disclose more information on costs and what a family will actually pay, and what we use tuition for
- implement technologies to achieve efficiencies, where possible
- focus on how students learn — we may have the wrong model
- engage faculty in problem solving

As for the government, some next steps should be:

- provide new grant money to promote access
- recommit to need-based aid principles
- target federal aid on need, not on merit
- resist the temptation to legislate the cost issues
- help change family perceptions about saving
- continue to encourage savings from the state level

And finally, suggested next steps for the College Board include:

- continue to provide a forum for discussion
- help institutions form partnerships with industry
- assist institutions in enrollment tasks through products and services
- spearhead partnerships for a media blitz on the importance of

saving, the importance of college, and the possibilities of college
- continue to tackle the savings disincentives in IM
- work with other associations to study the long-term impact of educational debt
- continue to work on the disclosure model
- continue to study the impact of the Taxpayer Relief Act of 1997 on IM and on college-going in general
- continue to disseminate materials on responsible borrowing through the CollegeCredit® program

Appendix A

List of Participants

Institution	Name	Title
Agnes Scott College	Stephanie Balmer	Director of Admissions
Amherst College	Joe Paul Case	Dean of Financial Aid
Arts & Science Group	David Strauss	Principal
Barnard College	Susan Lee	Senior Associate Director, Financial Aid
Beloit College	Alan McIvor	Vice President, Enrollment Services
Bentley College	Katherine Nolan	Director, Office of Financial Assistance
Berklee College of Music	Pamela Gilligan	Director of Financial Aid
Boston College	Frank Campanella	Executive Vice President
Boston College	Robert Lay	Dean of Enrollment Management
Boston College	Bernard Pekala	Director of Financial Aid
Boston University	Thomas Rajala	Director of Admission
Boston University	Barbara Tornow	Executive Director, Office of Financial Assistance
Boston University	Ryan C. Williams	Director of Financial Assistance
Bowdoin College	Walter Moulton	Director of Student Aid
Bradley University	Scott Friedhoff	Associate Provost for Enrollment Management
Bryn Mawr College	Nancy Monnich	Director of Admission and Coordinator of Financial Aid
Butler University	Richard Bellows	Director of Financial Aid
California Institute of Technology	David S. Levy	Director of Financial Aid
California State University, Long Beach	Gloria J. Kapp	Director, Admissions and Financial Aid
Carleton College	Jon Nicholson	Associate Dean of Admission
Carleton College	Stuart Perry	Associate Director, Student Financial Services
Carnegie Mellon University	Michael Steidel	Director of Admission
City University of New York	George Chin	University Director, Student Financial Assistance
Claremont McKenna College	Georgette R. DeVeres	Associate Dean, Director of Financial Aid
Consortium on Higher Education (COFHE)	Katharine Hanson	President
Colby College	Lucia Whittelsey	Director of Financial Aid
Colgate University	Mary Hill	Dean of Admission
Colgate University	Marcelle Tyburski	Director of Student Aid
College Board	Cynthia Bailey	Executive Director, Education Finance Services
College Board	Carol Barker	Vice President of Associational Affairs and Secretary of the Corporation
College Board	Mike Bartini	Director, Financial Aid Services
College Board	Frederick Dietrich	Senior Vice President, Programs and Development
College Board	Arthur Doyle	Vice President for Field Services and Corporate Marketing
College Board	Lawrence Gladieux	Executive Director for Policy Analysis

College Board	Hal Higginbotham	Vice President, Student Assistance Services
College Board	Jack Joyce	Manager, CSS Communications and Training
College Board	Kathleen Little	Executive Director, Financial Aid Services
College Board	Kathleen Payea	Manager, CSS/Financial Aid PROFILE and Need Analysis Requirements
College Board	Bradley Quin	Executive Director, Admissions, Enrollment and Information Services
College Board	Donald Stewart	President
College of Saint Catherine	Pamela Johnson	Associate Dean and Director of Financial Aid
The College of Saint Scholastica	Becky Urbanski-Junkert	Vice President for Admissions
Colorado College	Laurel McLeod	Vice President for Student Life
Colorado College	Libby Rittenberg	Faculty Assistant to the President
Colorado College	Jim Swanson	Director of Financial Aid
Colorado School of Mines	William Young	Director of Enrollment Management
Convent of the Sacred Heart	Mary Jemail	Director of College Guidance
Cornell University	Tom Keane	Director of Financial Aid
Cornell University	Nancy Meislahn	Director of Admissions
Cornell University	Don Saleh	Dean of Admission and Financial Aid
DePauw University	Anna Sinnet	Director of Financial Aid
Drake University	Thomas Willoughby	Dean of Admission
Duke University	James Belvin	Director of Financial Aid
Dwight-Engelwood School	Miguel Brito	Director of Guidance and Testing
Eastern Nazarene College	Martin Tice	Vice President for Enrollment Management
Embry-Riddle Aeronautical	Carol Cotman-Hogan	Director of Admissions
Emory University	Julia Perreault	Director of Financial Aid
Emory University	Dan Walls	Dean of Admission
Furman University	Benny Walker	Vice President for Enrollment
Georgetown University	Patricia McWade	Dean of Student Financial Services
Glenbrook North High School	Lois Mazzuca	College Counselor
Goucher College	Barbara Fritze	Vice President for Enrollment Management
Hackley School	Peter Latson	Assistant Director, Upper School
Hamilton College	Kenneth Kogut	Director of Financial Aid
Harvard and Radcliffe Colleges	James Miller	Director of Financial Aid
Harvey Mudd College	Patricia Coleman	Dean of Admissions and Financial Aid
Hinsdale South High School	Frank Palmasani	Counselor
Illinois Wesleyan University	Lynn Nichelson	Director of Financial Aid
Indiana University	Bill Ehrich	Associate Director, Student Financial Assistance
Indiana University	Terry Whitehill	Assistant Director, Office of Admissions
John C. Fremont High School	Laurice "Penny" Sommers	College Counselor
Johns Hopkins University	Robert Massa	Dean for Enrollment Management
Kalamazoo College	Marian Conrad	Director of Financial Aid
Kalamazoo College	Joellen Silberman	Dean of Financial Aid and Enrollment
Knox College	Terry Jackson	Director of Financial Aid

The Lawlor Group, Inc.	John Lawlor	President
Lehigh University	William E. Stanford	Director of Financial Aid
Loyola College	Mark Lindenmeyer	Director of Financial Aid
Loyola Marymount University	Joseph Merante	Associate Vice President for Academic Affairs
Macalester College	David Busse	Director of Financial Aid
Macalester College	Michael McPherson	President
Maguire Associates	Mary Ann Rowan	Vice President and Director of Midwest Operations
The Mercersberg Academy	William R. McClintock, Jr	Director of College Counseling
Miami University	Diane Stemper	Director of Financial Aid
Michigan State University	Thomas A. Scarlett	Director, Office of Financial Aid
Middlebury College	Robert Donaghey	Director of Financial Aid
Mount Holyoke College	Jane Brown	Dean of Enrollment
Mount Holyoke College	Kimberly Condon	Director of Financial Aid
NACAC	Patrick O'Connor	President
NACAC	Joyce Smith	Executive Director
NACUBO	James Morley	President
NASFAA	Marty Guthrie	Director of Governmental Affairs
Nassau Community College	Evangeline B. Manjares	Assistant Dean
National Commission on the Cost of Higher Education	Bruno Manno	Executive Director
NEISD/Robert E. Lee High School	Cynthia Monaco	Guidance Counselor
North Carolina State Education Assistance Authority	Steven E. Brooks	Executive Director
Norfolk Public Schools	Pamela Kloeppel	Senior Coordinator, Guidance
North Park University	John Baworowsky	Vice President for Admission and Financial Aid
Northern Virginia Community College	Carol Mowbray	College Coordinator of Student Benefits and Support Services
Northwestern University	Rebecca Dixon	Associate Provost of University Enrollment
Oberlin College	Howard Thomas	Director of Financial Aid
Oakton Community College	Evelyn Burdick	Executive Director of Institutional Relations
The Ohio State University	Natala Hart	Director of Financial Aid
The Ohio State University	Scott Healy	Director of Undergraduate Admissions
Paideia School	Virginia Rose	Director of College Counseling
Pitzer College	Abigail Parsons	Associate Vice President, Admission and Financial Aid
Pitzer College	Arnaldo Rodriguez	Vice President for Admission and Financial Aid
Pomona College	Patricia Coye	Director of Financial Aid
Pomona College	Bruce Poch	Dean of Admissions
Roosevelt University	Mary Hendry	Vice President for Enrollment Management
Rutgers University	John Brugel	Director of Financial Aid
Saint Mary's College	Mary Nucciarone	Director of Financial Aid
Saint Mary's University	Barry Abrams	Vice President for Enrollment Management

Saint Michael's College	Jerry Flanagan	Vice President, Admission and Enrollment Management
Sallie Mae Education Institute	Jerry S. Davis	Vice President for Research
Samuel Gompers Vocational Technical High School	Andrew Gooden	Student
Scannell and Kurz, Inc.	James Scannell	President
Scottsdale Community College	Ray Steiner	Director of Financial Aid
Scripps College	Patricia Goldsmith	Dean of Admission and Financial Aid
Skidmore College	Marylou Bates	Director of Admissions
Skidmore College	Sandy Baum	Professor of Economics
Skidmore College	Kent Jones	Dean of Enrollment
Skidmore College	Robert Shorb	Director of Financial Aid
Smith College	Maureen Mahoney	Dean of the College
Smith College	Myra Smith	Director of Financial Aid
Southern Illinois University	Pamela Britton	Director of Financial Aid
Southwestern University	Paul Gilroy	Director of Financial Aid
Stanford University	Cynthia Rife	Director of Student Awards
State University of New York	John Curtice	Assistant Vice Chancellor for Student Affairs and Financial Aid
State University of New York at Binghamton	Christina M. Knickerbocker	Director of Student Financial Aid and Employment
Swarthmore College	Laura Talbot	Director of Financial Aid
Syracuse University	Christopher Walsh	Director of Financial Aid
Taylor High School	Guy Oliphint	Student
Texas Christian University	Michael H. Scott	Director of Scholarships and Student Financial Aid
Thomas Jefferson University	Thomas Coyne	Director of Admissions
Trinity University	George Boyd	Executive Director of Admissions and Financial Aid
University of Arizona	Phyllis Bannister	Director, Student Financial Aid
University of Arizona	Lori Goldman	Director, Admissions Office
University of California, San Diego	Richard Backer	Assistant Vice Chancellor, Enrollment Management
University of Chicago	Michael Behnke	Vice President for Admissions and Financial Aid
University of Colorado, Boulder	Jerry Sullivan	Director, Office of Financial Aid
University of Connecticut	Dolan Evanovich	Associate Provost for Enrollment
University of Georgia	Nancy McDuff	Director of Admission
University of Maryland, College Park	Linda Clement	Assistant Vice President and Director of Undergraduate Admissions
University of North Carolina	Mary Garren	Associate Director, Scholarships and Student Aid
University of North Carolina	Shirley Ort	Associate Vice Chancellor and Director of Scholarships and Financial Aid
University of Notre Dame	Joseph Russo	Director of Financial Aid
University of Pennsylvania	William Schilling	Director of Student Financial Services

University of Pittsburgh, Bradford	Michael Heater	Dean of Admissions and Enrollment Management
University of Puget Sound	George Mills	Vice President for Enrollment
University of Puget Sound	Steven Thorndill	Director of Financial Aid
University of Richmond	Cynthia Bolger	Director of Financial Aid
University of Rochester	Andrea Leithner	Director of Financial Aid
University of St. Thomas	Marla Friederichs	Director of Admissions
University of San Diego	Judith Lewis-Logue	Director of Financial Aid
University of Southern California	Joseph Allen	Vice Provost for Enrollment and Dean of Admission and Financial Aid
University of Southern California	Morton Schapiro	Dean, College of Letters, Arts, and Sciences
University of Southern California	Catherine Thomas	Associate Dean of Enrollment Services and Director of Financial Aid
University of the Pacific	Lynn Fox	Associate Dean of Enrollment Services
University of Utah	Angela Wimmer	Program Manager, Scholarships
Upper Arlington High School	Jim Blosser	College Counselor
Vanderbilt University	David Mohning	Director of Student Financial Aid
Vassar College	Michael Fraher	Director of Financial Aid
Vermont Student Assistance Corp.	James Wolynec	Member, Board of Directors
Wake Forest University	William Starling	Director of Admission and Financial Aid
Wake Forest University	William Wells	Director of Financial Aid
Washington College	Kevin Coveney	Vice President for Enrollment Management
Washington College	Jeani Narcum	Director, Office of Student Aid
Wellesley College	Elizabeth Kim	Senior Associate Director of Financial Aid
Wellesley College	Janet Lavin-Rapelye	Dean of Admission
Wellesley College	Kathryn Osmond	Director of Financial Aid
Wesleyan University	Edwin Below	Director of Financial Aid
The Westminster Schools	Nancy Beane	College Counselor
The Westminster Schools	Juan Egues	Director of Financial Aid
Wheaton College	Robin Randall	Associate Dean of Student Financial Services
Williamette University	Todd Hutton	Vice President of Academic Administration
Williamette University	Leslie Limper	Director of Financial Aid
Williams College	Philip Wick	Director of Financial Aid
Wofford College	Susan McCrackin	Director of Financial Aid
Consultant	Deb Thyng Schmidt	

Appendix B

College Scholarship Service Council, 1997-98

Donald A. Saleh, Chair
Dean of Admissions and
　Financial Aid
Cornell University

Georgette R. DeVeres,
Chair-Elect
Associate Dean, Director of
　Financial Aid
Claremont McKenna College

Steven E. Brooks, Past Chair
Executive Director
North Carolina State
　Education Assistance
　Authority

Miguel Brito
Director of Guidance and
　Testing
Dwight-Englewood School

Joe Paul Case
Dean of Financial Aid
Amherst College

Andrew Gooden
Student
Samuel Gompers Vocational
　Technical High School

Gloria J. Kapp
Director, Admissions and
　Financial Aid
California State University,
　Long Beach

**Christina M.
Knickerbocker**
Director of Student Financial
　Aid and Employment
State University of New York
　at Binghamton

David S. Levy
Director of Financial Aid
California Institute of
　Technology

Evangeline B. Manjares
Assistant Dean
Nassau Community College

William R. McClintock, Jr.
Director of College
　Counseling
The Mercersburg Academy

Susan McCrackin
Director of Financial Aid
Wofford College

Cynthia Monaco
Guidance Counselor
NEISD/Robert E. Lee High
　School

Carol Mowbray
College Coordinator of
　Student Benefits and
　Support Services
Northern Virginia
　Community College

Lynn Nichelson
Director of Financial Aid
Illinois Wesleyan University

Guy Oliphint
Student
Taylor High School

Thomas A. Scarlett
Director, Office of Financial Aid
Michigan State University

Michael H. Scott
Director of Scholarships and
　　Student Financial Aid
Texas Christian University

Myra B. Smith
Director of Financial Aid
Smith College

William E. Stanford
Director of Financial Aid
Lehigh University

James M. Swanson
Director of Financial Aid
Colorado College

Howard Thomas
Director of Financial Aid
Oberlin College

Ryan C. Williams
Director of Financial
　Assistance
Boston University

65

Appendix C

Financial Aid Standards and Services Advisory Committee, 1997-98

Edwin Below, Chair
Director of Financial Aid
Wesleyan University

Youlonda Copeland-Morgan, Vice-Chair
Director of Financial Aid and
  Associate Dean of Admission
Harvey Mudd College

David Charlow
Director of Financial Aid
Columbia University

Mary Garren
Associate Director
  Scholarship and Student Aid
University of North Carolina,
  Chapel Hill

Stanley G. Hudson
Director of Financial Aid
Massachusetts Institute of
  Technology

Walter Moulton
Director of Student Aid
Bowdoin College

Mary Nucciarone
Director of Financial Aid
Saint Mary's College

Donna Palmer
Director of Financial Aid
Loyola Marymount University

Bernard Pekala
Director of Financial Aid
Boston College

Elaine Rivera
Director of Financial Aid
Tulane University

Roberta Stevens
Associate Director of
  Financial Aid
Vanderbilt University